Instructional
COACHES
and the
Instructional
LEADERSHIP TEAM

We would like to dedicate this book to our families for supporting us along the way and to the great instructional coaches that we have worked with over the years. D. T. S. & G. S.

Instructional
COACHES
and the
Instructional
LEADERSHIP TEAM

A Guide for School-Building Improvement

DEAN T. SPAULDING
GAIL SMITH

A Joint Publication

CORWIN
A SAGE Company

FOR INFORMATION:

Corwin
A SAGE Company
2455 Teller Road
Thousand Oaks, California 91320
(800) 233-9936
www.corwin.com

SAGE Publications Ltd.
1 Oliver's Yard
55 City Road
London, EC1Y 1SP
United Kingdom

SAGE Publications India Pvt. Ltd.
B 1/I 1 Mohan Cooperative Industrial Area
Mathura Road, New Delhi
India 110 044

SAGE Publications Asia-Pacific Pte. Ltd.
3 Church Street
#10-04 Samsung Hub
Singapore 049483

Printed in the United States of America.

A catalog record of this book is available from the Library of Congress.

978-1-4522-2638-5

Acquisitions Editor: Arnis Burvikovs
Associate Editor: Desirée A. Bartlett
Editorial Assistant: Kimberly Greenberg
Project Editor: Cassandra Margaret Seibel
Copy Editor: Erin Livingston
Typesetter: Hurix Systems Pvt. Ltd.
Proofreader: Susan Schon
Indexer: Jean Casalegno
Cover Designer: Michael Dubowe
Permissions Editor: Karen Ehrmann

This book is printed on acid-free paper.

SUSTAINABLE FORESTRY INITIATIVE
Certified Chain of Custody
Promoting Sustainable Forestry
www.sfiprogram.org
SFI-01268

SFI label applies to text stock

12 13 14 15 16 10 9 8 7 6 5 4 3 2 1

Contents

Preface

If you are a district administrator, principal, or school leader and want to improve the quality of instruction in each and every classroom, where do you begin? You begin with this book. This book will provide you and your Instructional Leadership Team (ILT) with a step-by-step guide to improve each and every one of your teachers by using the talent and expertise from within your own learning community. Imagine improving the academic achievement of your students at no additional expense! All you have to do is recognize and identify the endless amount of talent and expertise you already have in your building through the use of instructional coaches.

Each chapter of this book not only provides school leaders with important information on how to go about implementing instructional coaching but also provides materials to help with the step-by-step implementation process. At the end of each chapter you will find Self-Study Activities and data collection forms and instruments to be used by school leaders and instructional coaches. These forms have already been field-tested and will allow you and your staff to seamlessly collect the vital data and conduct the day-to-day activities to maximize the effect of your building's instructional coaches.

In addition to end-of-chapter materials, you will also find a wide variety of materials and instruments at the end of the book. These too have been field-tested and designed by instructional coaches for collecting various forms of formative and summative data to improve classroom practice and student achievement. In a time when school buildings are being closed and teachers terminated for poor student performance, the need for high-quality classroom instruction has never been greater. However, how a school goes about improving instruction is an entirely different matter altogether. Traditionally, improving classroom instruction has been left up to the building principal. Principals have typically addressed this need by conducting classroom observations, giving staff formative feedback, and providing professional development opportunities; however, a principal's ability to visit classrooms is quickly diminished by the vast numbers of noninstructional issues he or she has to deal with on a daily basis. These noninstructional issues severely limit the amount of time and impact a principal can have on instruction in the classroom. In many cases, this lack of administrative presence has created a gap in trying to improve classroom instruction, particularly in low-performing schools. In order to address this gap, many schools have turned to employing instructional coaches.

WHAT IS AN INSTRUCTIONAL COACH?

An instructional coach (IC) is an on-site professional developer who works directly with teachers and staff on how to go about implementing research or evidence-based strategies and techniques into their everyday classrooms. While instructional coaches may sound similar to literacy coaches, the instructional coach takes a more "generalist" approach, many times working with teachers one-on-one on a wide variety of content from mathematics to science. A successful instructional coach is a unique individual. They must be skilled in a variety of roles. They have to be a public relations guru, a communicator extraordinaire, a master organizer, and, of course, an expert educator.

USING AN INSTRUCTIONAL LEADERSHIP TEAM APPROACH

Even though they may have an IC in the building, many schools find that they don't necessarily make the gains in student achievement they were expecting. Research suggests that when it comes to using an IC, many ICs unfortunately fall victim to the same distractions that keep many principals out of the classrooms. In order to gain the most impact from having an IC in your building, a larger team effort has been recommended. The role of the school principal and teaching staff is critical in providing the ideal environment for instructional coaches to work and be successful. This team approach is often referred to as the Instructional Leadership Team or ILT. The purpose of this book is to provide a guide or framework for the school principal, staff, and the instructional coach to create a more effective environment for the instructional coach to work in and be successful.

OUR RESEARCH WITH INSTRUCTIONAL COACHES

For the last fifteen years, we have been working with ICs in one form or another. Many of our research and evaluation projects incorporate some aspect of ICs to improve classroom instruction and ultimately increase student achievement. Most recently, we have conducted a study of 13 instructional coaches in low-performing elementary school buildings and worked with the ICs to provide technical assistance as well as to document day-to-day progression and professional growth of these instructional coaches and the teachers they worked with. All of this research has formed the foundation for this book, allowing it to take on a unique approach that separates it from other instructional coaching books currently on the market. This book is different from other books on the market because it recognizes the importance of the school community: the building principal, the school staff, and the instructional coach. Using a "journaling approach," the book provides the point-of-view of all three of these stakeholders and therefore can be read and enjoyed by all members of the school community. This dialogue is critical in showing the different perspectives, their views of instructional coaching, and how such a good idea can oftentimes be derailed.

In our research, journaling and interviewing instructional coaches as they worked through the day-to-day challenges in their buildings became a staple for trying to get a better insider's view of the life of an instructional coach. We learned so much from this process that we felt it was an essential component to our work and needed to be represented in the book. In order to maintain confidentiality, the journal entries have been fictionalized; however, they still focus on a critical seed or kernel for which they were written. In addition, we think the journal entries provide a realistic perspective that could not be captured through any other method. They provide a unique backdrop against the chapter's narrative.

When we started working with our instructional coaches, we wished we had a book like this to hand out on our first day. We spent weeks—months, in some cases—navigating the choppy waters, trying to guide our new instructional coaches through the many challenges they faced on a daily basis. We were also there to celebrate the successes. Don't forget about that! It is very important to stop and take a minute to congratulate oneself when some action yields an unexpected success. We often think about how much more support we could have given our instructional coaches and how much further they could have gone improving the instruction in their buildings. While this book may be intended for instructional leadership teams (ILT) or coaches who are relatively new to the idea of instructional coaching (or are just exploring the idea), it also is intended for those instructional coaches who have been in the position for some time. They, too, will be interested in exploring new ideas and avenues to take their work to the next level. We wish you all great success.

—D.T.S. & G.S.

CHAPTER OVERVIEWS

Chapter 1: "I'm So Glad You're Here!" The First Day as an Instructional Coach

Every instructional coach has a first day. Some first days, however, are better than others. Chapter One focuses on the first day of being an instructional coach and the challenges instructional coaches often face when taking this position. This chapter provides an overview as to the different perspectives the building principal, teachers, staff, and the instructional coaches themselves can have about the role and responsibilities of the instructional coach. Early on in their careers, many instructional coaches are often derailed by the misperceptions those in their building have about their position. As in the case described in the chapter's journal entries, the building principal, pressed for time and resources, may be the biggest culprit. This chapter provides a framework for four key steps that need to be conducted in order for an instructional coach to be successful: establishing an Instructional Leadership Team (ILT), establishing a job description for the instructional coach (IC), establishing the role and responsibilities for the IC, and establishing an action plan for the IC.

Chapter 2: The Instructional Coach and the Instructional Leadership Team: A Unique Approach

In this chapter, you will learn more about the inner workings of the ILT and how the IC works with the team. You also will read about the two sets of priorities in a school building and how a school principal cannot address all of these priorities at once. This inability to address everything creates a gap, particularly in the area of working with teachers and providing feedback, and is filled by the role of the instructional coach. You also will learn about how the ILT works and some strategies the team can use to identify areas in need of improvement within the school building.

Chapter 3: Refocus and Start Again! The Instructional Leadership Team Supporting the Instructional Coach

Unfortunately, instructional coaches' best efforts might not necessarily yield the desired results. While it may seem logical for an instructional coach to first work with the lowest-performing teachers in the building, research has shown that this is not the most strategic move for an instructional coach. Information from this chapter comes directly from our work with instructional coaches, documenting their challenges and how they worked to overcome them and be successful. The chapter also provides ideas and information for how the IC can serve as an extension of the ILT, working in classrooms and with teachers to improve classroom instruction. This chapter also provides the IC and the ILT a framework for analyzing data and making data-based decisions.

Chapter 4: The Day-to-Day Work of the Instructional Coach

One of the unique features of being an instructional coach is that one rarely has the same day twice. Because of the complex set of roles and responsibilities of the IC, even though one may plan the day, lots of obstacles stand in the way. This chapter provides the IC with strategies for identifying promising teaching practices in the building and establishing a network for teachers' exemplary practices that can be shared and observed by others in a nonjudgmental manner.

Chapter 5: An Idea for the Day: Strategies and Ideas to Encourage Engagement Between Teachers and the ILT

After the initial work has been completed, there is still much to do. This chapter provides guidance to the instructional coach about ways to work with teachers in the building and contains over 40 different ideas used by ICs to engage and work with teachers.

Chapter 6: Assessing Individual and Group Strengths: Strategies for Working With the Resistant Teacher

Unfortunately, not every teacher in the building will greet the instructional coach with open arms. In fact, some might even be resistant to learning about new evidence-based instructional strategies or introducing these strategies into their classrooms. Working with resistant teachers is a real challenge for today's instructional coaches. This chapter focuses on presenting ideas and activities for the IC to follow when working with the resistant teacher.

Chapter 7: Changing Teacher Practices Through Classroom Field-Testing: The ILT's Role

In this chapter, the IC learns how to work with all types of teachers through field-testing practices in their classrooms. This chapter is dedicated to providing instructional coaches with a framework to help the IC assist teachers in investigating various instructional strategies and practices in their classroom and then reflecting on whether those practices were effective for increasing student learning.

Chapter 8: The ILT's Role in Changing Teacher Practices Buildingwide

This chapter focuses on how instructional coaches can combine the professional development and action research to create a powerful new way to improve teacher practices. Based on the work of Guskey (2002), this approach provides a model as well as technical information to instructional coaches in order to create a learning community where instructional coaches introduce and demonstrate evidence-based practices and teachers research the effectiveness of these practices in their classroom. Then instructional coaches and teachers come together for in-depth discussion and dialogue.

Chapter 9: A New Coach in Town! The ILT's Role in Training New Instructional Coaches

With the success of an instructional coach comes a need for more coaches in the district. This chapter focuses on the techniques and strategies that can be used to cultivate talent and develop the next cohort of instructional coaches.

Chapter 10: Toolbox for the Instructional Coach: Examples of Surveys, Protocols, and Tools

This chapter contains materials and supplements developed on-the-job by the instructional coaches we worked with.

Acknowledgments

We would like to thank Courtney Wayman, Jen Dilorio, Kristina Osborne-Oliver, and Craig Zinkiewicz for assisting us with researching our book.

PUBLISHER'S ACKNOWLEDGMENTS

Corwin would like to thank the following individuals for taking the time to provide their editorial insight and guidance:

Ann Dargon, Assistant Superintendent of Schools
Westport Community Schools
Westport, MA

Kathy Ferrell, Instructional Coach
Excelsior Springs Middle School
Excelsior Springs, MO

Kay Kuenzl-Stenerson, Literacy Coach—Reading Specialist
Oshkosh Area School District
Oshkosh, WI

Tanna H. Nicely, Assistant Principal
Dogwood Elementary
Knoxville, TN

Cathy Patterson, 5th Grade Teacher
Walnut Valley Unified School District
Walnut, CA

Kathryn Silva, Director of Student Services
Ashland Public Schools
Ashland, MA

About the Authors

Dean T. Spaulding is currently an assistant professor at the College of Saint Rose in Albany, New York, where he teaches educational research and program evaluation. Dr. Spaulding is the former chair of the Teaching Evaluation SIG for the American Evaluation Association. He also has been a professional evaluator/researcher for fifteen years and has in-depth experience serving as an evaluator on multiple state- and federally funded projects. More specifically, he has conducted evaluation for programs focusing on K–12 settings, the use of technology in the classroom, and working in the area of teaching and learning with at-risk youth populations. At the government/state agency level, Dr. Spaulding has conducted research and provided programmatic feedback for New York State Department of Education, New York State Department of Public Health, and the New York State Office of Mental Health (OMH). Dr. Spaulding also is one of the authors of *Methods in Educational Research: From Theory to Practice* (2006, Jossey-Bass Wiley) and the author of *Program Evaluation in Practice: Core Concepts and Examples for Discussion and Analysis* (2008, Jossey-Bass Wiley) and *Action Research for School Leaders* (2012, Prentice Hall). Dr. Spaulding is also a consultant at Z Score Inc. (dspaulding@zscore.net).

Gail Smith, a native of Brooklyn, New York, received her BA and MS at State University College at Oneonta, NY. She received her master's degree in education administration at the University at Albany, State University of New York. Her thirty-six-year career at an upstate New York urban school district included positions as a teacher, assistant principal, principal, assistant superintendent, and deputy superintendent of schools. In 1988, Gail was one of five finalists for New York State Teacher of the Year. After retiring, Ms. Smith worked for two years as an administrator at two different schools on Native American reservations in Arizona and New Mexico. She returned to her home district in July 2008 to work as a consultant and mentor for their Instructional Leadership/Instructional Coaches project. She also is the proud mother of three children. This is her first of many publications.

"I'm So Glad You're Here!" **1**

The First Day as an Instructional Coach

What a day! I've had crazy days before at this school but never anything like this. Teaching has never been easy. I've been there with the frustrations, pressures, and uncertainty, but I always knew what the mission was and where I fit in with that mission. I had twenty-two fourth graders, and it was my job to make sure they learned everything, stayed safe and happy, and worked toward proficiency or better on their standardized tests. It was a tough job for sure, but I always knew what the job was and so did everyone else. But not today!

Today, I started a new job at school, and I have never been so confused, so lost, or so scared in my entire professional life. I came home more worried and upset than ever before, and I am starting to rethink this entire thing.

After ten years in the classroom, I was happy but stuck. I wanted a new challenge, a new perspective. I wanted to make a difference beyond my classroom, and, yes, I wanted a little recognition for all my skills and good work. I did not want to become an administrator. Not me! No way! That is an important role for sure, but I wanted to keep closer to my role as teacher, plus a little more. They posted the position of Instructional Coach and I jumped at it, but now I have no idea what I said "Yes" to.

When I got to school this morning, I headed for Principal Sander's office. It was weird not going to my old classroom and thinking of someone else in there setting up my bulletin board. I guess I'll have to get over that. I knocked on Principal Sander's door and when invited in, I sat down, hoping to discuss the day ahead.

"I'm glad you're here!" she said with a big smile. "There is so much to do, and I can use all the help I can get. I know we've talked a little about all you will be

doing this year, but I wrote down some things I think you might do, just to get us started. We can refine and revise as we go along. I can't tell you how happy I am to finally have some help around here. Well, here is the list. Why don't you check out your new office, and I'll meet you in a half hour in the library for the opening faculty meeting. I am so glad you are here!"

With that, her phone rang and I took it as my cue to leave the office. I headed to my new office, a converted book storage room across the hall; not a bad space— just not my space. Not yet anyway. I sat down with my coffee and started reading the list Principal Sanders had handed me. By the time I got to the third item, I was questioning everything about this decision I had made to become the school's instructional coach. The list she had made included the following tasks:

1. *Assist with student discipline as needed*

2. *Standardize test administration*

3. *Cover office when principal is out of the building*

4. *Visit classrooms and teacher consultation*

5. *Serve as parent liaison*

6. *Organize testing materials and supplies*

7. *Serve as school rep on ELA curriculum committee*

Is this what an instructional coach is supposed to be doing? What did these things have to do with instruction? This sounds like an assistant principal's job description and more. I don't want to be an administrator.

This was clearly not what I had signed on for. I wasn't sure what my new job was, but I knew this wasn't what I thought it was. How could I handle all of these tasks and still have time to really make a difference in the academic achievement of our students? The only task on the list I thought did belong was number four. How could I tell Principal Sanders that I just didn't agree that assisting with student discipline was a part of my new role? After all, she is my boss and I am supposed to be helping her, right? What a mess I have made for myself! How am I ever going to get it straightened out?

Mrs. Skyler Sanders, School Principal
Journal Entry: September 6

Today was the first day of school. It is always exciting, but this year, I think is going to be particularly good. I welcomed the students back to school at a morning assembly and had the first meeting with Mrs. Wright, my instructional coach. Although this is only my second year here as principal, I know Mrs. Wright will do an excellent job as an instructional coach. She is a highly effective teacher who understands classroom instruction and the literacy program we are now using here. Most important, she is very well respected by the other teachers. I think she will do a superb job.

We have never had an instructional coach here before at Franklin Elementary. I am not exactly sure what an instructional coach is or what one does. But when the district office called me over the summer and said that they had grant monies to fund an instructional coach for the next three years and did we want one, I certainly wasn't going to refuse. Who refuses help like this? Besides, I also know that the principals in the other elementary buildings were getting instructional coaches. Hopefully, she will be able to take some of the load off my desk and free me up so I can go in and conduct more observations of teachers.

During our meeting today, I gave Mrs. Wright a list of her new job responsibilities. A lot of them were things that I know I am supposed to be doing, but I honestly can't find the time. It is going to be a big help having her around to take some of the load off. I imagine that after awhile she will be able to get into the classrooms and help teachers directly, but for now I need her to help me as much as possible, to shoulder some of this responsibility I have on a daily basis. I am so glad she is here. This is going to be a great school year!

> **Ms. Amanda Shaffer, Veteran Teacher**
> **Journal Entry: September 6**

Today was the first day of school. At the assembly this morning, Principal Sanders announced that Mrs. Wright was going to be our instructional coach for our building this year. Principal Sanders said that many of the other elementary buildings also got an instructional coach and that these coaches are supposed to help us improve our instruction. I have been teaching for 20 years. Why didn't someone ask me if I wanted to be an instructional coach? I think I do a pretty good job with these students, so I don't know how much help the instructional coach will be. If she thinks she is going to come into my room and tell me what to do, she'd better think again. Some of the other teachers were talking about it in the break room this afternoon. They said that we'd better be careful; they had heard that this instructional coach was going to be a spy for administration and that Mrs. Wright was reporting directly to the principal. In fact, several of the teachers said that the instructional coach had already met with the principal first thing this morning. I will be nice to her, but I am not going to let her in my room. She can't help me. All in all though, I guess it was a good first day. It feels good to be back. Now, I just have to make it through one more school year. Can't wait until June . . .

WHAT IS AN INSTRUCTIONAL COACH (IC)?

Instructional coaches have recently become a popular strategy for schools in need of improvement (Makibbin, & Sprague, 1993). While there are many titles used to refer to instructional coaches (e.g., school leader, instructional support specialist, curriculum specialist, etc.) one thing remains certain—their purpose. The purpose of the instructional coach (IC) is to work directly and indirectly with teachers, staff, and the building principals to improve the effectiveness of classroom instruction and increase student learning, performance, and overall achievement; however, the IC cannot and will not be successful working solo in a school building. Researcher studies suggest that it takes a school community working with its IC to be successful in improving classroom instruction and eventually student performance.

THE INSTRUCTIONAL COACH—THE EARLY EXPLORER

In some ways, being an instructional coach is like being an early explorer, setting sail for uncharted waters. While there is certainly research and literature to guide instructional coaches, the process or steps an instructional coach takes to be successful still remains virtually unexplored. Ultimately, the coach has to be willing to try out certain strategies and practices to determine what works. In some ways, the instructional coach has to be a researcher, conducting small, informal experiments; studying what strategies or techniques are the most effective for changing teachers' classroom practices; and improving classroom instruction. While the uncertainty of this job may be frightening, for those who want to reflect critically on practice and collaborate with others, the opportunity is quite different from years of teaching in a classroom.

Many times, administrators introduce an instructional coach to a school, believing that an instructional coach is the secret ingredient needed to fix a low-performing school (Joyce, Showers, Murphy, & Murphy, 1989). While having an instructional coach is certainly a step in the right direction, an effective instructional coach is not something that happens by accident or chance. In fact, experts note that this type of success only happens with a lot of planning, time, commitment, support, and strategizing (Saphier & West, 2010).

In the case depicted in the earlier journal entries, several steps should have taken place to avoid what transpired in the school. Presented below are the steps:

- Step One: Establish an Instructional Leadership Team (ILT) (e.g., principal, IC, teachers, and staff).
- Step Two: Establish a job description for the IC.
- Step Three: Establish the role and responsibilities for the IC.
- Step Four: Develop an action plan for the IC.

STEP ONE: ESTABLISH AN INSTRUCTIONAL LEADERSHIP TEAM (ILT)

In further examining this situation, it is important to remember that the principal is still the instructional leader of the building; however, this creates a real challenge for principals trying to improve the instructional level in the building. We all acknowledge the fact that in order to improve instruction, one has to enter the classroom to observe it. No matter how much the principal reassures a teacher that the observation and feedback is informal and for improving practice, the teacher believes that he or she is being judged. The IC, being a third party (and not in an administrative position), can function differently in this situation.

Take another minute to reexamine the three journal entries at the beginning of this chapter. Then ask yourself: How did one great idea get so misunderstood so quickly? The obvious answer is that there was no clear understanding or agreement about the instructional coach's role prior to its launch. That is the obvious answer, but not the entire answer. The bigger issue surrounds a concept that is usually seen in a very positive light: Help is coming! Help was arriving for this school in the form of a new position—an instructional coach; however, in a situation such as this, where help arrives undefined, those who need the assistance will define it through their own lens, regardless of the relevance to its intended goals. Help can be seen as a welcomed gift, but it also can be received with suspicion and an assumption of judgment, as shown in the journal entries above. Unsolicited help can be greatly resented, feared, and sometimes even sabotaged. Those who welcome the help will, if permitted, focus it on their immediate needs while ignoring (for the most part) what the original intent of the help was for.

In this scenario, help was seen as coming from one, and only one, outside source—the instructional coach. Somehow this help would magically be able to fix all the problems in a school building. We all know that *real* help comes from the facilitation of problem solving by those most closely involved. Real help comes not as a Band-Aid but as an entire first aid kit, providing the practitioners with the right tools, opportunities, and information at the right time. Real help comes from within the group that requires it.

Despite how the help was perceived by the various players in this situation, we do know that the instructional coach model works—and works well when properly implemented and supported (Knight, 2007). We also believe it only works when it is an important component in a broader Instructional Leadership Team (ILT). The ILT includes not only the IC, but also the support of the school leader and faculty. The ILT is a team of three as shown here in Figure 1.1.

As you can see from Figure 1.1, the ILT is made up of three main components: the school administrator, the IC, and teachers/staff. It is these three entities working together that identify issues related to instruction in the building (as well as determine methods to address these issues). In the next chapter, you will see how the IC works with the ILT to accomplish these feats.

The IC can, and must, work within this team of three to develop a fluid, responsive, proactive, research-based process that is present throughout the fabric of the school community. Within this framework, the role of the

Figure 1.1   The Instructional Leadership Team

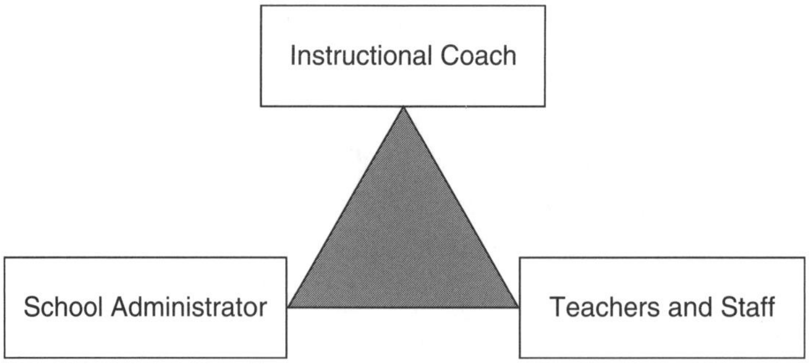

IC can be defined, revised, and redefined as needs arise. If this is done, it will help to ensure that this position will be a benefit for everyone involved.

STEP TWO: ESTABLISH A JOB DESCRIPTION FOR THE IC

As you read the earlier journal entries, you may have asked yourself the question, why didn't the school district develop a job description for the instructional coach? Could all of this confusion been prevented? This is a good question, and in most cases, the answer would have been "yes." A job description is a written statement that conveys key characteristics, requirements, and responsibilities for a position. While job descriptions will vary greatly depending on the nature of the position, all job descriptions should have some essential elements. A carefully constructed job description should have the qualifications one needs to hold the position, a general list of task and responsibilities, salary range, and benefits. It also should clearly identify the persons to whom the IC would report.

As you can see from the journal entries, having all members of the school building aware of the role and responsibilities of the IC is a pivotal component to the overall success of this initiative. Without it, things could become counterproductive for all members of the school community, preventing the attainment of the primary goal of improved students' learning and academic achievement.

The role of instructional coach is and must always be tailored to meet the specific and evolving needs of the school, its faculty, and its principal. There is no "one size fits all" boilerplate job description that will cover every nuance of this component of the Instructional Leadership Team. Because of the complexities of the IC position, developing a job description that accurately reflects the depth and breadth of work an IC may conduct is both critical as well as challenging. Despite these challenges, there are some general guidelines that districts can embrace as the overarching blueprint within which all the tailoring may occur.

STEP THREE: ESTABLISH THE ROLE AND RESPONSIBILITIES FOR THE IC

While the role and responsibilities for the IC would most likely be embedded in the job description, it is important that these components are carefully crafted. Take a look and examine for a moment the role and responsibilities in the example job description below. Which of these descriptors meet your perception for an IC?

Purpose Statement:

An instructional coach position was created to improve classroom instruction and enhance student achievement.

Roles

- Mentor to teachers
- Model to teachers
- Instructional leader
- Data analyst
- Teacher liaison (teacher-administrator)

Responsibilities

- Demonstrates knowledge about effective curricular instruction and assessment practices
- Helps teachers design curricular activities
- Monitors effectiveness of classroom strategies
- Provides quality interactions with teachers through frequent classroom visits
- Models best practices for teachers in their classrooms
- Coaches teachers to improve student learning and provides feedback in a nonevaluative manner
- Analyzes and reports student achievement data
- Uses student achievement data to drive instruction
- Plans professional development
- Meets with grade-level teachers on a regular basis (e.g., to review student work, deal with areas of concern, and plan upcoming units)
- Uses and models use of technology as an instructional tool to support student learning

- Assists in the selection of instructional and professional materials

- Maintains open and effective lines of communication with all parties

- Has both the willingness and the ability to actively lead change initiatives with hopes of inspiring new and better ways of instruction and learning

Nature of Work
Under the direction of the principal, the primary role of this individual is to act as an agent of change, leading initiatives that will systematically result in higher levels of engagement and thinking among students and teachers.

Duties and Responsibilities

- Is directly involved in designing curricular activities and assessments that inform instruction

- Models and supports effective teaching strategies and techniques in a nonevaluative manner

- Facilitates ongoing dialogue about instructional practices

- Is informed of current research in learning across all areas and acts as an informational resource for teachers at the building level

- Effectively integrates the use of technology as an instructional tool to support student learning

- Assumes responsibility for supporting new teachers at the building level

When launching any new initiative that is not already part of the historic fabric of the organization, it is important to give clear parameters indicating what the position can and will include. It is equally important to delineate what the position does not include in its roles and responsibilities. The challenging and resource-strapped circumstances our schools often face make it tempting to use this new resource—the IC, without an immediate and daily responsibility for a class of students—as the first person to be called upon to fill other unmet needs within the building. While we understand the temptation, we strongly suggest that this should be avoided completely. If the instructional coach becomes the person on call, it will be far more difficult to define the actual role within the school community.

Faculty perception of the purpose of the instructional coach is vital to the success of this initiative. If the instructional coach is seen through the lens of other roles and responsibilities, the important perception becomes diluted, skewed, and damaged. The effectiveness of the instructional coach will be reduced to a large degree. Of course, there will always be emergency situations that require everyone to pitch in and help, but the instructional coach cannot become the permanent "first responder" for the building.

Here are some suggested descriptions of what an instructional coaching position should *not* include:

- The IC is not a substitute teacher, administrator, paraprofessional, nurse, lunch supervisor, and so on.
- The IC is not a faculty evaluator.
- The IC is not the assistant principal, discipline dean, or office supervisor.
- The IC is not a clerical assistant.
- The IC is not a resource teacher, remedial subject area teacher, or special education teacher; although, they may certainly have expertise in any of these areas.
- The IC is not part of the administration.

Having this list available for all faculty as the ILT begins its work should help clear up a lot of confusion, reduce the amount of misinformation, prevent unrealistic expectations, and allay a great many fears, suspicions, and concerns.

STEP FOUR: DEVELOP AN ACTION PLAN FOR THE IC

For many instructional coaches new to the position, knowing where to begin is not only a frightening thought but one that may seem almost insurmountable. This lack of knowing where to start can often derail even the most focused IC, since the IC can be misdirected by request for help by others. In close examination of the journal entries, this may have contributed to some of the frustrations felt by Mrs. Wright, the new IC. Not knowing her role and responsibilities completely as an IC, coupled with the fact that she had no real game plan, created a less-than-perfect day for this instructional coach.

An action plan is a sort of blueprint that will provide even the most experienced IC with a more accurate perspective of the need within the building and also a clear starting point of where to begin. The action plan should be developed by the ILT. The building principal, IC, and staff should all contribute to this process of strategically determining where the IC should focus time, energies, and available resources.

The ILT may go through a series of steps to determine what needs to be included in the action plan. The ILT may conduct an in-depth analysis of student performance data as part of this process. They may even conduct a trend analysis, examining student performance at the same grade level over a number of years to determine areas where students are not meeting the minimum benchmarks. This new knowledge would then help direct the IC's efforts, and the IC would focus his or her efforts on working with teachers in the specific areas identified via the in-depth data analysis.

In other cases, the action plan may be more micro in that it focuses the IC's efforts on a specific set or cohort of teachers who need to improve some aspect of their current classroom instruction. Action plans also can focus on a series of professional development areas. In this case, the IC would be responsible for carrying out the professional development and then pushing into classrooms to extend and support what teachers learned in the training.

Not only is the action plan versatile, but it also is flexible in that it can be modified and abridged on an as-needed basis. The action plan would be a working document used by the ILT to reflect upon and refine as the team works along with the IC to create progress in the school building. In future chapters in this book, you will learn more about the action plan and how, as an IC, you and your ILT can use this document to optimize your role and effectiveness in improving teacher practice.

SUMMARY

Assistance for improving schools comes in many forms. In this chapter, you read about how a very good initiative to help improve instruction went astray. The instructional coach was uncomfortable about what her role entailed and, because of this, was taunted through the day with memories of her old position as a teacher in the building. The principal, already overloaded on the first day of school, also did not know the role or purpose of the instructional coach and, therefore, found an immediate way for the instructional coach to help out. In not knowing the IC's role, the principal selected some initial activities for the instructional coach; however, only one was aligned with what Mrs. Wright, the instructional coach, thought her duties should be. And then there was the teaching staff. They, too, had not been informed about the instructional coach position; many of them, no doubt, were just hearing about it for the first time that day. They were suspicious and judgmental and believed that the instructional coach was a sort of spy for the building principal. Unfortunately, these misperceptions are shared by many teachers in districts that implement an instructional coach model without first carefully developing a shared perception among the stakeholders in the building as to what the instructional coach's role and purpose will be. Unfortunately, this entire misunderstanding will eventually impact the depth and breadth of the work that the IC can do and greatly impede the effectiveness of the initiative overall.

A job description is a key element to any position; however, it is an even more critical element for the success of an instructional coach. Because there are so many possibilities (and distractions) for the instructional coach position, it is important to have a job description in place not so much for the coach but for others in the school community to understand the role and responsibility of the coach. If all members are aware of the purpose of the instructional coach, situations like the ones shown at the beginning of this chapter will most likely not be an issue. While job descriptions vary greatly, one of the most important factors when creating (or refining) a job description for an instructional coach is that it is a collaborative effort. Another is that its development is always focused on the goal—improved academic achievement for all students via strong and consistent instructional leadership at all levels.

███

Self-Study Activity #1

For the Instructional Coach:

Pretend for a moment that you are instructional coach Mrs. Wright (or Mr. Wright). Pretend that you started your first day as the IC and everyone in the building had the same perception of your role as you did. How might your journal entry look now? Take a few minutes and write a journal entry about what the first day of school was like for you. Reexamine your journal entry and come up with a list of things that you believe would need to be in place in order for your journal entry to look the way that it does and not like Mrs. Wright's at the beginning of the chapter.

_____

_____

_____

_____

_____

_____

_____

_____

_____

_____

For the Building Principal:

On the first day of school, Principal Sanders had a meeting with staff—what a missed opportunity to inform staff about the purpose of the IC. Knowing what you now know about an IC, prepare some key speaking points about how you would describe the purpose, role, and responsibilities of your building's newest member.

_____

_____

_____

_____

_____

_____

For the Teachers or Related Staff:

Nothing is more powerful than a person's first impression. Knowing what you now know about instructional coaches, take a few minutes and write a new teacher journal entry. Pretend you are interested in working with the IC. On what types of activities or areas would you see the IC working with you and other instructional faculty in the building?

_____

_____

_____

_____

_____

_____

_____ ▪ ▪ ▪

The Instructional Coach and the Instructional Leadership Team

2

A Unique Approach

Mrs. Skyler Sanders, School Principal
Journal Entry: September 25

I feel like I am on some sort of roller coaster. Two weeks ago, I started off the year believing I finally had help, and I was thrilled. Then I began to see a very different picture. My help vanished before my eyes, and in its place was a whole new puzzle; a new challenge, new idea, and a whole new set of potential problems.

The faculty meeting on opening day—not a success! The new IC position roll-out was met with . . . well, let's just say the response was underwhelming. That is, what little response there was other than glares, silence, and a few mumbled comments—all negative. Even the IC looked confused and worried.

I went back to my office and scribbled some notes—questions, really—about what this all meant, what went wrong, and what I should do next. I did some serious thinking, followed by some research on this whole IC thing and that led me to some thoughts about my own role. More about that later, but when I next met with the IC, I found that she too had been on a roller coaster ride and was just as concerned and worried as I had been. After we hashed it all out, we knew one thing for sure: we had to start over and do something very different in order to make this all work for our school, starting with the faculty. We realized that we could not be a team of two, not if we wanted this to work. If this was going to be successful, everyone had to be an equal member of this leadership team. Everyone had to have a share in this and work in ways that were traditional for us and in new ways that were outside the proverbial "box" of ideas we had implemented in the past. We had to take some risks and encourage the faculty to do the same. We needed everyone to suspend their disbelief at the possibility that this new idea was not just another new idea that would come and go with nothing much changed in the process. We realized that we had to open up the process of leadership and slowly and carefully invite the faculty in. It was obvious now that we needed everyone's help in defining this new role and everyone's participation and support in getting it launched and keeping it going. This could not be a top-down, "we have a new plan and we are going to tell you what it is" project. This was a "snowball project"—one that starts very small, slowly rolling downhill, gathering more and more involvement from more and more colleagues as we moved forward.

First, we had to look for the next opportunity to talk with the faculty. The obvious target was our next schoolwide meeting, which was scheduled for today. Then we had to plan a meeting that was completely different from the format we've always followed. We needed a meeting that was a consensus session with shared leadership and real decision-making power. "Well," I thought, "is that all?" Seriously, this had to be different; it had to be inclusive, and it had to work on a lot of levels. We planned and presented an activity in which the faculty worked to develop the basic job description for the instructional coach. In about a half hour, the faculty had participated in an activity that had real and immediate results. They were empowered, and it seemed to get everyone's attention. (Well, almost everyone.) Some are still suspicious about all this and some are certainly still reluctant or apathetic about it all, but there was a definite shift in the participation level at the meeting after this activity. I'm determined to make sure that they see that what they decided is what we are doing as we begin to grow this leadership initiative.

Then we focused the discussion on data. We redefined data *as* tools *rather than* bludgeons. *We came up with a list of nontraditional sources of data. The conversation centered on an activity in which everyone wrote down three words to describe data and listed three sources of data. We talked about the descriptive words, most of which seemed to take a negative tone. Many of the words described a punitive, frustrating, or relentless process. I explained that we were going to look at data from now on in a new way. We focused on and discussed the topic of action research, and I gave a brief explanation of how I believe it works. We talked together, in general terms, about how data can and should be used as a tool, a road map, and a guide as well as in its usual capacity as measure of achievement. I then introduced three charts, each one listing a problem we have discussed every year at this school without ever resolving it. They are three issues I personally would love to never have to discuss again! I told the faculty that together we would use data, come up with solutions based on the data/information we collected, and resolve these three issues by November 1! Well, that got everyone's attention, and this time I do mean everyone! We brainstormed on what data/information we would need to resolve each of these problems and decided who would collect what data, with everyone having an assignment. We would come up with a plan of action for each problem based upon what the data told us.*

After the buzz died down (positive buzz, I believe), I took a few moments to explain that this new meeting format and the focus on data as active research were part of what I intended to be a "new normal" for our faculty and that I planned for everyone's support and participation in academic leadership from now on. I also explained that I was reclaiming my own role as instructional leader and that I would make classroom visits my major focus of every day. I assured everyone that the IC would never be called upon to act in an evaluative role and encouraged everyone to think of ways this new opportunity could match their own ideas of coaching.

I'm not sure, but I think I even heard a little bit of very quiet applause as the meeting broke up. I know I saw a lot of happier, more hopeful faces and witnessed some animated conversations as people left the cafeteria. Mrs. Wright looked happier, too, and surely a bit more relieved, but I still have to make sure I am responsive to her needs and concerns. I know we have to move slowly and carefully and thoughtfully. I know I have to continue to work on changing my own mindset about leadership. I know this won't be easy for anyone. Yet today, for the first time in a long time, I really think we can get there!

Mrs. Janice Wright, Instructional Coach
Journal Entry: September 25

Well, I got over a big hurdle last Monday: the schoolwide meeting following that first crazy week. After my first meeting with Mrs. Sanders and that first faculty meeting, I was such a bundle of emotions: sad, confused, afraid, disappointed—you name it. I knew I had to do something, but what? Everyone knew what my new job should be and yet no one really did know. Everyone had a plan for me—a different plan! Not one of those plans sounded remotely like the one we had talked about over the summer when all the new ICs got together. I know that the IC position is supposed to evolve organically based on my building's academic strength, needs, and goals, but nothing I heard during week one sounded remotely like what examples we had listed as we talked in August. I lost a lot of sleep, and at first, I just thought of how I was going to handle all of this, and then I decided to see Mrs. Sanders again for an honest talk. "Maybe I'm not the person for this job," I thought, "or maybe I am all wrong about what this job really entails. Maybe I am the right person to be the IC." I just didn't know, but I knew I couldn't figure this all out alone. We had to talk—the principal and I first and then all the faculty together. We needed to find, if not common ground, at least the same beginning place. We need to talk, all of us, honestly, about what a coach is in this circumstance and why we need one here at our school. Given all the confusion and suspicion I had already encountered, I frankly didn't have much hope of getting this off to a better start. I just knew we had to do something and try to make this work. I feel it has so much promise if we can all agree to try this together.

We needed to have a "do over" now that we had a better idea, a common idea, of what this role should be. We did something that would change the conversation not only about the IC position but about the main focus of our mission—academic excellence and effective instruction. We found a way to start to get faculty back in the boat with us. Trust! We began to build trust! We knew this could only happen slowly, by admitting we don't know it all and by leading through consensus. This was huge, much more than simply figuring out what my job was going to be.

I felt great because I could use what the faculty decided on as my guide for the next month, getting me in to classrooms to work on things we had all agreed to. Soon I'll be asking the faculty to determine ways in which they can coach, too.

Together, the faculty worked to develop a coaching plan, to define the instructional coaching role, and to build the trust necessary to deal with all these issues in a safe coaching environment. We began a process that will actually use data to solve some problems . . . together! I'm not sure, but I think I even heard some quiet applause as the meeting broke up.

Will this work? Who knows? Now I have some guidance, and it came from my colleagues. We had a meeting where many people began to take on leadership roles. We have at least started the discussion about data and research in ways that, if we are successful, will help us all to welcome them as tools, supports, and road maps to success. I know that I am more hopeful than I was a week ago, and I know that people are talking about that meeting even today. The conversation has started. Maybe I'll get some sleep now!

> **Mr. Christopher Todd, Veteran Teacher**
> **Journal Entry: September 29**

New year, new idea, same old story. That's for sure what I thought when Mrs. Wright talked to us at the opening-day faculty meeting about this new IC position. We've been down so many roads with so many new programs and nothing really ever changes. So I was, truthfully, barely listening when this came up. I had too much on my mind, really: the new reading series, the eight special education students included in my room this year (never so many before), all the things I had to do to get the room ready, and worry about how my daughter was doing at her first day in high school. I just was not focused on whatever this "next new thing" was going to be. I didn't have room in my head for all of this. Sure, I know Mrs. Wright; I worked with her in our team teaching project. She's a good person and I think she is a really good teacher, but so am I! I don't need a coach. I think it is good that the new teachers will get some help, but I'm OK on my own.

Two days later, we were reminded about our first schoolwide meeting. "Well, here we go," I thought, "down another path that leads nowhere." Another session of looking at the test results from last spring and talking about what it all means. It's just an endless conversation that gets us nowhere, so I was dreading it. But I have to say, I was pleasantly surprised.

First off, it was the first meeting I've been to lately where the principal wasn't up front talking to us or at us. For another thing, we actually got to decide a few things—or at least I think we did. We talked about the IC job again, what it isn't and what it might be. We also talked about a lot of things I have never thought of as data. I'll reserve judgment of this whole "action research thing," but if we solve the copy paper problem and reduce PA announcements by November 1 of this year, I'll be a happy camper.

Bottom line, I feel like the principal and the instructional coach are really trying to change the process and not just fix us.

I don't know. Maybe this is just more of the same, but I'm beginning to think maybe it isn't. All I know is that our schoolwide meeting was different, and I didn't hear so much griping about it in the faculty room. No matter what, I sure hope to have more meetings like that one. First time I've felt heard in a long, long time!

THE PRIORITIES OF A SCHOOL LEADER

While the building principal remains the instructional leader of the building, you can see from the journal entries in Chapter One that the principal faces a pile of responsibilities, challenges, tasks, and other crises on a daily basis. Many building principals struggle with trying to decide what has to be done that very moment and what can wait for another day. Unfortunately, getting into classrooms to observe teachers gets put on the back burner all too often. The activities or priorities a building principal is responsible for can be broken down into two levels or types: Priority One and Priority Two. Priority One responsibilities pertain to the safety and welfare of all those who are in the building to learn, work, or visit. As you can see in Figure 2.1, Priority One issues form the base of the school system—without Priority One in place, learning cannot be possible.

Presented in Table 2.1 is an overview of Priority One issues. Missed buses, office referrals, and suspensions can consume a busy principal who has the best intentions in getting to classrooms and improving instruction for all students.

But what is Priority Two? Priority Two is the main purpose for the school's existence; it is the mission of the learning community and the purpose for which it has been established. Priority Two is the academic achievement of all students at the highest levels. As the leader of the school, along with providing a safe and healthy school environment, the principal's main role is that of instructional leader; that is the principal's charge. It is and it must be the driving force behind the principal's every effort; however, it is often lost in the details of the day-to-day operation of a school. Principals are often without support staff, buried in their offices by the demands of everyone and everything within their school community.

Figure 2.1   Priority One and Priority Two Issues

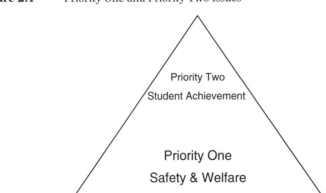

Table 2.1   Examples of Priority One and Priority Two Issues

Examples of Priority One Issues	Examples of Priority Two Issues
School suspension	Examining and implementing research-based curriculum and best practices
Bus duty	Parent conferences
Student attendance	Item analysis and in-depth examination of student performance on state tests
Making sure substitute teachers are hired	Developing and implementing high-quality programming before school, after school, for enrichment, and so on
Office referrals	Creating effective classrooms and learning environments throughout the building
Teacher absenteeism	Observing classrooms and providing in-depth formative feedback to teachers on a regular basis
Building maintenance issues	Working with teaching staff to conduct action research projects in the classroom
Dealing with grievances	Focusing on differentiated instruction

Student discipline, bus schedules, the lunch program, required reports, parent concerns and complaints, community outreach, and meetings—of every description—compete for the principal's attention, leaving little time to focus in any depth on Priority Two issues on a consistent basis.

PRIORITY TWO AND STRONG INSTRUCTIONAL LEADERSHIP (SIL)

Strong instructional leadership (SIL) is often mentioned as one of the components without which significant improvement in student achievement cannot be attained or sustained (Green, 2010; Guthrie & Schuermann, 2010; Marzano, Waters, & McNulty, 2005). According to Green (2010), SIL focuses on teaching and learning, where "effective leaders facilitate the application of current knowledge in learning and human development" and "use data to make instructional program decisions that meet the needs of all students" (p. 10). In order to have SIL, an instructional support team is needed. This team includes both the principal (as the instructional leader) and the entire faculty and staff. Presented in Figure 2.2 is an example of a building where strong instructional leadership (and an instructional support team) is present.

Figure 2.2   Optimal Addressing of Priority One and Priority Two Issues

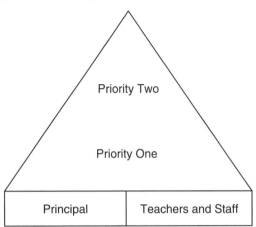

Here the principals, the teachers, and school staff are all on board, jointly sharing the same visions to optimize instruction. In this example, the instructional team is able to address all the Priority One and Priority Two issues in the building. In order to do this, all members of the instructional leadership team (i.e., the school) have to be present, participating fully in their roles and responsibilities. If one of the groups does not fulfill their responsibilities, SIL is no longer fully present and the priorities begin to suffer.

As discussed earlier, one of the common challenges faced by school principals today is the overwhelming amount of Priority One tasks that they are responsible for in a given day. Spending a great deal of time focusing on Priority One tasks causes Priority Two tasks to suffer (see Figure 2.3), and the foundation for learning is no longer supported because the teachers and staff and the principal are not equally focused on supporting *both* tasks.

Figure 2.3   Unbalanced Priority Strategy

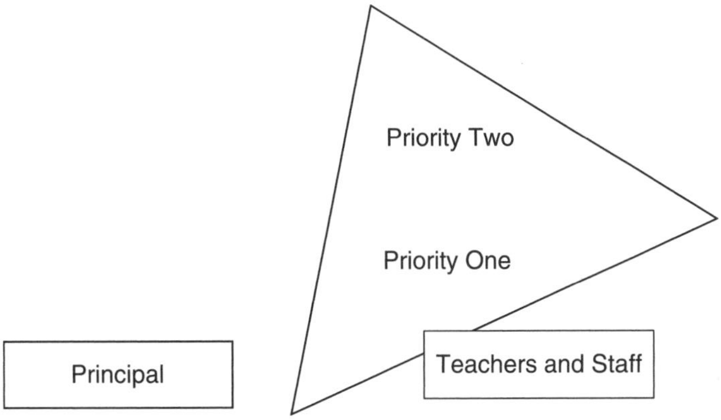

Unfortunately, one of the first activities that principals tend to cut back on is going into classrooms and observing teachers. Studies show that only one-third of teachers report being observed on a regular basis by their building principals after receiving tenure.

As shown in Figure 2.4, the instructional coach (IC) helps address the gap left in the instructional leadership team model when principals, busy with all the other demands of the position, cannot or do not go into the classrooms. The missing support caused by the principal's lack of presence (while dealing with other issues) is filled by the IC.

Instructional coaches can identify areas of need and serve as a resource for addressing concerns and weaknesses throughout the building. The instructional coach encourages the building principal to be more active in the instructional leadership role and facilitates faculty efforts to serve as coaches as well (Killion & Harrison, 2006; Samuels, 2008). The instructional coach promotes best practices and encourages action research as common strategy for all staff. Action research is a formal investigation of the real problem, whereby an individual or group identifies the problem, consults past research, implements a treatment, and gathers data to determine if the intervention was effective. An action *plan* doesn't place a large emphasis on research methodology in determining what works. If the intervention works, then so be it; the participants move on to the other issues in the building that need solving. In action *research*, the researcher is vested in research methodologies and gives great care to understanding data collection methods and will select those that will best examine the research question or hypothesis under investigation.

The instructional coach serves as a conduit for information, ideas, and materials consistent with the school's mission and efforts to improve. The instructional coach serves as a facilitator, an ombudsman, a supply sergeant, an adult educator, a respected and respectful colleague, an active

Figure 2.4   Principal, Instructional Coach, and Teachers and Staff

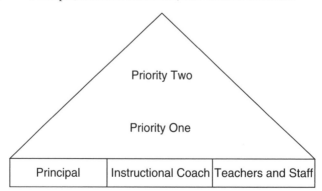

listener, and a mirror reflecting the mission back to each faculty member so they may be reminded, renewed, and refocused when the need arises.

SIL done consistently and actively improves instruction to a far greater degree than any individual professional development course or set of materials could. The instructional coach is a vital component in that SIL recipe. As instruction becomes more effective and academic, needs of all students are met, real and significant academic achievement results, and the school truly progresses toward its stated goals.

SIL is more than a Band-Aid or a specific repair; it reaches past the symptoms of inconsistency and ineffectiveness and, as a united team, works to repair, redirect, and reshape the effort at the heart of the process—teaching and learning in each individual classroom. Within a comfortable and collegial environment, healing begins; commitments are made; relationships are built; ideas are nurtured; efforts are supported; talents are discovered or rediscovered; change takes place; and the results are a source of pride for all involved.

The road to SIL and sustained academic improvement is not without its detours, construction delays, traffic jams, and every other metaphorical challenge you might wish to add. Research does agree that without strong instructional leadership, however, the journey will end (if it ever does) at a destination no one would choose. In many cases, the IC cannot be successful working solo in the school building. As noted by Saphier and West (2010), it takes a coordinated effort to create an environment for the IC's work to be most effective. As shown in Figure 2.4, this new team, consisting of the principal, IC, and faculty and staff, is known as the instructional leadership team (ILT).

THE INSTRUCTIONAL LEADERSHIP TEAM (ILT)

In an effort to provide this much-needed coordination, many school buildings are turning to an instructional leadership team (ILT) to help guide the IC and ensure the biggest impact for their effort. To better understand how the IC works within the ILT, it is best to have a better understanding of how the ILT should and *should not* function.

AN EQUAL AND SHARED VOICE

While the principal still remains the instructional leader of the building, the IC and other team members also play a critical role. In order for the team to run effectively, the team should establish some basic ground rules. The first, and perhaps the most important, is equal voice. This means that no team member (not even the school principal) has more bargaining power than any other member. The ILT should be a place where diverse ideas and helpful, thought-provoking discussions and conversations can and do take place.

In addition, the ILT also should be representative of the school building, school culture, and overall mission. Teachers and staff who sit on the ILT should represent the school; this can be done by making sure that all grade levels and content areas are represented and that the ILT is not seen as an exclusive group or clique with a preset agenda. Such perception of the ILT by teachers and staff will not only discount the potential good work that the ILT could do in the future, it will also hinder the current work of the IC to improve instruction. In some cases, the ILT may want to consider having a parent representative on board in order to provide more of a bridge between the school and the parent community.

BASIC STEPS FOR THE ILT

The process used by each ILT will be (and should be) different depending on the school itself and the instructional issues that need to be addressed. While it is virtually impossible to develop a standard approach, there are some basic components or steps that the ILT should think about incorporating into its processes. These steps also are important, since they provide a natural base for the work of the IC.

Step 1 and Step 2: Analyze Data and Identify Instructional Areas in Need of Improvement

One element that the ILT should try to avoid is selecting an issue that is not a high priority. Using data to drive school improvement is one common method used by school administrators and ILTs to avoid this problem. Engaging in the process outlined below in Figure 2.5 will also help your ILT to avoid being derailed from the efforts the team should be focusing on. In Step One, the ILT selects relevant school data and begins to examine it more closely. While these data are often student performance data from high-stakes assessments, they can also include (but are not limited to) school report card data, student behavior data, or school attendance data. One method used for data analysis is called *disaggregation.* In this process, which ties in to Step 2 (identifying areas of instruction that require improvement), team members would begin to examine data (e.g., student performance results) by common variables. In education, these variables often include gender, general education versus special education status, ethnicity, and free/reduced lunch.

Figure 2.5   Steps for the ILT

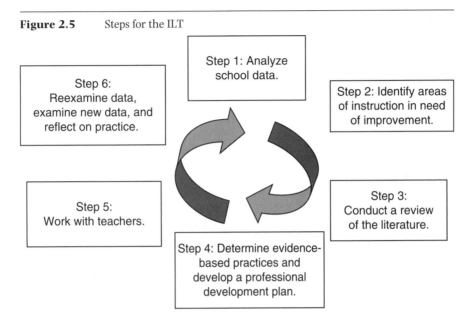

Step 1: Analyze school data.

Step 2: Identify areas of instruction in need of improvement.

Step 3: Conduct a review of the literature.

Step 4: Determine evidence-based practices and develop a professional development plan.

Step 5: Work with teachers.

Step 6: Reexamine data, examine new data, and reflect on practice.

For example, is there a difference in performance on the state 7th grade mathematics assessment between males and females or among students by ethnicity? This disaggregation of data can be done on the total score of an assessment or by individual items or clustering of items. For example, an analysis that examines the type of items 7th grade students missed on the latest high-stakes assessment in mathematics might reveal that students missed a large number of items pertaining to proposal reasoning. The ILT could conduct a trend analysis, examining the performance of 7th graders on the mathematics exam for the past five years. Keep in mind that each year contains a different group or class of students flowing through the system and taking the 7th grade mathematics assessments; however, these data can be very valuable in gaining insight to questions such as

- How are our 7th graders performing on the annual state mathematics assessment since we implemented the new math curriculum five years ago?
- What are common areas where 7th graders have gaps in mathematics knowledge across the last five years?

These questions help identify potential areas in need of improvement. And, while it may not initially seem like it, the role of the IC during Step One is critical. In many cases, because of their busy schedules, the principal and members of the ILT may not have the time, the ability, or the access (e.g., if parents served on the team) to gather the specific data needed to perform the analysis. Therefore, the IC may find it necessary to access these particular data points for team members so that discussion and data analysis can seamlessly occur. In many cases, the first analysis of the data creates additional questions, thus requiring more data to be collected for further in-depth analysis. For example, while the first analysis made by the ILT may consist of examining state assessment data, the team may find it helpful to also have student attendance data. This second layer of analysis also would allow team members to determine whether attendance is an underlying issue to student performance on the annual state assessment. If they find that there is a relationship, they may decide to address the issue surrounding low student performance on the state assessment differently with this new data being added to the equation. This deeper analysis is often referred to as *drill down* analysis and should be done until members of the ILT are satisfied that the data analysis has indeed provided them with an intricate (and hopefully more accurate) understanding of possible causes creating the issue in the data.

Step Three: Conduct a Review of the Literature

While Step Two in Figure 2.5 is critical to the overall improvement process, many school administrators and school-based improvement teams skip this vital component. In Step Three, the ILT should gather and critique the current research and literature related to the instructional issue they want to address in their building. In some cases, this literature may focus on discussing the possible contributors or reasons why teachers have a particular gap in their knowledge or instructional classroom practices. While this literature does not necessarily provide a course of action, it should not be discounted by members of the ILT but thoroughly examined and discussed to determine if these noted contributors also are present in their school building's current culture. In addition

Types of Analyses

Disaggregation Analysis—examining whether a difference exists in performance between two groups or variables

Trend Analysis—examining student performance at the same grade level or data collection point for a number of years in a row

Cohort Analysis—following the performance of the same group of students for several years in a row

Longitudinal Analysis—the same as cohort but for a longer period of time (10 years or more)

to reviewing this type of literature, the ILT also should be searching for evidence-based instructional practices that have research supporting their use in the classroom. It is important to ensure that the ILT is identifying evidence-based and research-based instructional practices. ICs may find themselves gathering and initially reviewing the research and literature on the topics and presenting the materials to members in order to provide an organized and seamless transition between the various steps presented in Figure 2.5.

Step Four: Determine Evidence-Based Practices and Develop a Professional Development Plan

In an ideal world, the ILT could identify a handful of evidence-based practices, present these practices to the faculty, and the faculty would instantly see the need for these new practices and seamlessly integrate them into the classroom the very next day. Unfortunately, the process doesn't quite work like that. Changing teacher practices and the use of professional development to create more effective classroom instruction is an ongoing body of work and research (Guskey, 2002). While such work for the ILT begins here at Step Four, Chapter 9 provides a much more detailed methodology for the IC working with teachers through a professional development model. At this point in the junction, the ILT can begin to engage in conversations and questions pertaining to how they are going to go about trying to change teacher practices. Questions at this level might sound similar to the following:

- What kind of professional development (PD) do teachers need in this area?
- What should the PD look like? Formal? Embedded?
- What does the literature on the subject say about student challenges that occur while learning this material?
- What are teachers' challenges with this topic and with delivering quality instruction on this topic?
- What does research say are evidence-based instructional practices or strategies that could be added to the current instruction to improve learning in the classroom for students in this area?

Step Five: Work With Teachers

What exactly the ILT decides and develops as a plan of action will greatly impact the direction and efforts of the IC. In some cases, the ILT might decide that the IC should begin to work with small groups of teachers to begin to model the new evidence-based practices they have identified from the review of literature. In doing so, the IC might suggest that the small group of teachers initially be those who are generally more receptive to new initiatives and teaching practices. This way, the IC can build a rapport with the most responsive teachers, build capacity and motivation around the new instructional strategies and practices, and use this momentum to increase interest in motivation with the other teachers in the building. (Specific techniques and models for how an IC most effectively and efficiently works with a wide range of teachers in a building to improve practice will be featured throughout this book.)

Step Six: Reexamine Data, Examine New Data, and Reflect on Practice

In this final step, the ILT continues its efforts to reexamine data as it emerges in order to determine the impact of the instructional practices. The ILT will critically review new data and make modifications (new or additional practices and PD) to the equation. In most cases, the IC would play a pivotal role in providing content for the new data analysis as well as needed modifications.

SUMMARY

The success of an instructional coach cannot happen in isolation. As noted by experts, the effectiveness of the instructional coach is largely dictated by the coordination established by the organization itself. While Priority One issues (e.g., school safety) are the foundation for providing a quality learning environment, the number of Priority One issues that need to be addressed by a school principal greatly impacts the principal in being able to observe classrooms and in providing constructive feedback for teachers regarding their instruction. Unfortunately, without the presence of instructional leadership, the quality of classroom instruction is compromised and student achievement is sacrificed. School administrators who create an instructional coach position in their building to address this problem without setting up the proper support of channels may be doing an even further disservice. The key to a strong instructional coach in the school building lies with the instructional leadership team. This team is made of the building principal, the instructional coach, teachers, staff, and, in some cases, a parent representative. The team acts as a single unit and follows a process whereby team members examine data, identify areas of instructional weakness in the building, develop professional development plans for groups and buildingwide initiatives, and then monitor through data the progress the effort is making. As an extension of the ILT, the IC works directly with teachers to provide the required professional development deemed necessary by the ILT in order to improve practice. How the IC goes about working with teachers depends on what is needed to be addressed as well as the interest of the teacher to improve practice. A whole host of strategies and practices can be used by the IC to achieve his or her goal. In future chapters, you will read and learn more about these strategies, which can be used by the IC to help facilitate the collaborative work of the ILT and improve student achievement.

■ ■ ■

Self-Study Activity #2

Prioritizing Shared Responsibilities

School Administrator:

Examine the list of Priority Two activities in Table 2.1 and create a list below of those activities that you *should* do as the instructional leader for your building. Notice that the key word here is *should.* Feel free to add any other activities to your list that do not appear in Table 2.1.

_____

_____

_____

_____

_____

_____

_____

_____

After you have completed this, place an asterisk (*) next to all of those Priority Two activities on your list that you don't have time to get to.

Instructional Coach:

Examine the list of items under Priority Two in Table 2.1 Using this list, create a new list of activities below that you believe are vital to reaching Priority Two in the building. Be sure to add any additional items of your own that aren't on the list.

_____

_____

_____

_____

_____

_____

_____

_____

Now, place an asterisk (*) next to all of those items on the list that you are comfortable with overseeing and feel that are part of your job as an instructional coach. Next, circle those items that have asterisks to indicate that you need further training or professional development in order to feel comfortable conducting these tasks.

Teacher/Faculty Member:
Examine the list of items under Priority Two in Table 2.1. Use those items and items of your own to create a new list of items that you believe will assist the building as a whole achieve Priority Two.

_____
_____
_____
_____
_____
_____
_____
_____

Now place asterisks next to all those Priority Two items that you would like to do but either can't get to because of time constraints or because you need assistance in order to accomplish these goals. Circle those items with an asterisk that you believe an IC could assist you with.

Compare and Share Analysis

When all the members of the instructional leadership team have completed the questions, compare lists and answer the following questions:

- Are there commonalities in what people have indicated for Priority Two?
- Are there Priority Two activities that school administrators and teachers feel are important but can't get to work on? If so, these are some of the first initial pieces that an instructional coach can do with the instructional leadership team.
- Are there items that teachers find valuable to the classroom but can't get to or items on which the IC needs further training? If so, these are some key components that school principals can use to support instructional coaches by directing them to appropriate professional development.
- Are there areas "that slip through the cracks," where everyone indicates that they are important, but no one has the time or the expertise to address them? If so, create a list of these areas and discuss them at the next leadership team meeting. Try to come up with some creative solutions.

Refocus and Start Again! **3**

The Instructional Leadership Team
Supporting the Instructional Coach

> **Mrs. Skyler Sanders, School Principal**
> **Journal Entry: October 24**

Dreading this next meeting of the ILT. We have committed to looking at data as it relates to our progress with reading, especially with the new reading program we have started working with this year. We did a data review last spring as we tried to set academic goals for the upcoming school year. Teachers worked hard, as they always do, trying to glean information from all this test score data and to make decisions that would benefit our students, but I remember how heavy the room felt! As I set up the school's results on the screen, there was a collective sigh; you could feel the disappointment with our less-than-spectacular results. It was pervasive. It was also obvious, by everyone's demeanor, that people were feeling attacked, blamed, and bludgeoned by the information. There was a definite feeling of "here we go again" as the discussion progressed. I got some good ideas from the meeting because these teachers are true professionals and they are always trying to turn failure into success, but none of us were sure what our plan really had to do with the information. It all seemed too general and unfocused.

Now we are looking at the data again, trying to see the information as evidence to be collected and examined. We're going to try and decide on what other sources of evidence might be of assistance to guide us and direct us throughout the year rather than to serve as a judgment in June, when it is too late to do anything about it all. I am hoping to build on the positive feedback from our initial activity in data-driven problem solving, which has resulted in a better system of copy paper distribution and a more peaceful transfer for students from classroom to cafeteria every day. I hope to turn the focus of that process to our academic needs, starting with the new reading program.

I'm hoping the new procedures I've committed to will turn the teachers away from the sense of futility they feel in these types of efforts and toward a sense of team building, problem solving, and scientific exploration. I think we may be able to change the tone of the conversation on the concept of the very purpose of data itself, from its traditional role of judgment to that of catalyst for progress. I hope . . . !

Mrs. Janice Wright, Instructional Coach
Journal Entry: October 24

OK, I am really nervous this week. Our next meeting is going to focus on data! That could make or break our new ILT. We've agreed, as a team, to look at the data on our reading progress again. I can't believe the teachers on the team have agreed to this, and I know some are dreading it, but we need to take another look, a different look, at all the evidence that will really show us how we are doing with this new reading program. It will tell us, if we do this right, what is working and what we have to change along the way instead of hitting us in June, when it is too late to do anything differently. The principal and I are trying to shift the focus of discussion on data from judgment to guidance; that's how we introduced the idea to the rest of the team and to the teachers who haven't joined us yet. If we hadn't done those data-collection projects last month, this never would have happened, I don't think; but teachers are really happy with the changes made to solve the copy paper issue and the halls are much quieter now when the classes go to the cafeteria. That little bit of success has made a crack in the wall as far as data is concerned. We don't even call it data *any more. It is* evidence!*

I'm trying to build a list of new and different potential sources of evidence to bring to the meeting, things we have never included in these conversations before, ideas that come from the faculty. So I've talked to teachers about the new reading program. I've asked each of them for ideas about how we will know what is working well and what needs to be changed. These discussions helped me develop a long list of ideas—everything from the time of day for the reading block (as it relates to student tardiness) to intercom usage to periodic vocabulary assessments to parent contact frequency. These are not the usual sources of data (oops, evidence) *that we usually discuss and examine. The conversations have also given me access into some classrooms I haven't been invited to before. I'm starting to be seen more now as a person to collaborate with rather than as an "administration spy." It's also given me lots of new ideas and information to contemplate, new questions to ask, and new paths to pursue.*

The meeting is in two days. I have a list of twenty-six new sources of evidence that we will need, and no one has mentioned data *in the last few days. This really could work. I hope! . . .*

Ms. Amanda Shaffer, Veteran Teacher
Journal Entry: October 25

Great! Just great! That new ILT is going to have a meeting tomorrow on our new reading program and we are going to discuss our state reading scores . . . again! We're all invited to the meeting but I am not going. The last thing I want to do after school is to listen yet again to how poorly we did in reading last year. I already know it, and I am tired of hearing it again and again. I am working hard to try and help the students to do better. These discussions never really change anything. Besides, we have a new reading program this year, and I have all I can do to figure that all out. Maybe this program will be the magic bullet we need. I'll just work on doing my best and hope it helps us all to do better this year.

On another note, Mrs. Wright, the new instructional coach, stopped by to talk about the new reading program. I thought she was going to push her way into my room, but all she wanted was to ask how things were going with it. I told her that so far I thought the program was OK but that I am not sure the reading block is at the right time of day. I have a lot of kids who get to school late and they miss a lot of reading instruction because of that. Mrs. Wright said that she would bring it up to this new ILT and include it as something we need to examine; she said it was evidence that we may need to help us know how the program is working and if changing the time might help. Maybe I'll stop by the meeting after all and add my two cents about the timing. But I am not staying if that same old data discussion starts! I hope this really will be a different kind of meeting. If it is, maybe I'll give another thought to signing on. I hope things can change. I hope. . . .

While the instructional coach (IC) certainly has autonomy over what he or she does on a daily basis, in many ways, the IC can be thought of as an arm or extension of the instructional leadership team (ILT). The IC carries out day-to-day activities in the classrooms, meeting rooms, and hallways of the building. These day-to-day activities should be aligned to the overall plan of action envisioned by the ILT; however, in the end, it is important to remember that all actions of the IC are ultimately driven by ILT.

HOW THE IC CARRIES OUT THE ILT'S PLAN

Since the ILT follows a data-based decision-making practice, the first thing examined by its members is data. While a further in-depth analysis of data and how to use it can be found later in this chapter, it is important to remember that the first step taken by the ILT is to examine data and make decisions about what needs to be improved. There are several decisions that can be made by members of the ILT based on their data analysis: selection and implementation of a new curriculum across the building, continuation of existing curricula, and providing professional development to specific grade levels or specific teachers—or all of the above.

SELECTION AND IMPLEMENTATION
OF A NEW CURRICULUM

If warranted, the ILT may decide that it is necessary to select and implement a new curriculum to improve student achievement. If this is the case, the IC will certainly have a lot of work to do. Implementing a new curriculum successfully takes a lot of work and planning. The first step that will have to be conducted by the ILT is to determine, as a team, what curriculum is best suited for the building and for the learning gap that is currently taking place. As part of this process, the IC can play an important role by helping members of the ILT to select a promising curriculum to implement as well as do some of the leg work in collecting research and information about potential curricula. In this situation, the IC can play an important role in helping to support the ILT team members, who are often busy with their other professional commitments. Members will rely heavily on the IC to not only gather information about the new curriculum but also to digest some of this initial information and weigh in on the curriculum.

As part of this process, the IC should do the following:

- Work with members of the ILT to both examine the data and brainstorm potential curricula that could be implemented to address the issues seen in the data.
- Reach out to other nearby districts or buildings that have similar issues to see what types of curricula they are currently implementing and to determine if they have been successful in meeting similar goals.
- Try to limit the ILT by focusing on two or three different programs or curricula for the IC to conduct further research on. Too many possibilities will only confuse matters and result in the delay of the timeline for moving forward.
- Contact curriculum publishers for potential reviews, copies of programs, or curricula.
- Examine as much research and literature as possible on the potential curriculum under review. Be sure not only to look at research provided by the developers and publishers but conduct a search for any independent research that might also be available.
- Conduct a thorough review of the literature about the potential curriculum and be able to present an overview to members of the ILT. Be sure to provide an overview of the program as well as research findings that would support its use.
- Be prepared to take down any follow-up questions posed by team members, and be sure to provide additional information at the next meeting to answer these questions and provide closer guidance before a decision by the ILT is made.

IC PROVIDING PROFESSIONAL DEVELOPMENT (PD) AND TECHNICAL ASSISTANCE

In addition to assisting the ILT in making sound, research-based decisions for selecting new curricula or programs, the IC will also have to play an important role in helping teachers adopt and adapt to the new curriculum and instructional practices. The IC should be prepared to help provide professional development, to help teachers and school staff understand the goals and objectives of the new curriculum or program, and to help them implement it correctly in the classroom.

There are two types of professional development. *Formal* professional development is when the district or building brings someone in from outside the school as a consultant to deliver training. It is usually a contractual obligation for the teachers to attend. *Embedded* professional development does not usually use an outside consultant; instead they use someone—such as the IC—from within the building. Embedded professional development takes place during common planning times for teachers and is usually done on a more individual, as-needed basis.

Depending on the situation, the IC may decide to provide teachers with embedded (or *traditional*) professional development. Using an embedded professional development model, the IC would provide training to teachers and staff in small group settings, perhaps by grade levels. Here, the IC would be responsible for overseeing the training and for providing teachers with the technical information necessary to implement the new curriculum with fidelity. In some cases, an external consultant might be brought in to provide additional training or technical support that goes beyond the jurisdiction of the IC.

Follow-up and job-embedded PD would also fall to the responsibility of the IC. In this situation, the IC would work directly in the classroom one-to-one with teachers, providing modeling as well as observation and direct feedback to help ensure that teachers were implementing all aspects of the new curriculum correctly on a day-to-day basis. Here, the feedback provided to the teacher by the IC is vitally important for improving the teacher's classroom practice and maintaining quality control for the research-based program. (How exactly the IC works with teachers in the classroom is discussed in more detail in later chapters.)

FEEDBACK FOR THE ILT

Even though the IC is quite busy during this process, the IC must also take time to provide formative feedback to the ILT. Keep in mind that this feedback is not specifically about individual teachers but is information that the ILT needs to make additional informed decisions. For example, let's say that the ILT has selected a new intervention for seventh grade students based on analysis of student performance for the past several years. As a group, the ILT decides to implement a new curriculum for seventh grade. Curricular materials and new textbooks are purchased, and the IC works with seventh grade teachers to provide initial group training followed by embedded training in each of the teachers' classrooms; however, as a result of engaging in this process, the IC discovers that many of the teachers also have deficiencies in other areas. This information is important to the overall improvement of classroom practice for the building and should be funneled back to members of the ILT. Again, depending on the situation, the ILT may decide teachers need additional professional development in other areas and may work to support the IC by seeing that these new issues are addressed as well.

PROFESSIONAL DEVELOPMENT FOR THE IC

While the IC plays an important role in providing quality professional development for teachers and staff, it is also important for members of the ILT to remember that the IC may, at times, need professional development as well. While the IC has a strong command over effective instruction in general, the IC cannot be an expert in all areas. At times, the IC will need to attend trainings as well as familiarize him- or herself with different resources and materials. Members of the ILT can help support the IC by knowing when the topics or issues that need to be addressed in the building are moving toward uncharted waters and by supporting the IC in seeking out additional opportunities to learn more and expand his or her repertoire. The ILT can further support the IC by ensuring that there are resources available. More specifically, the building principal should establish an annual budget line specifically for professional development and outside training for the IC. The principal should not only make the IC aware of this budget but allow the IC to manage the budget as he or she sees fit. Here are some possible ways the ILT can support the IC:

- Allow the IC to attend professional development or training conferences outside of the school setting
- Support the IC in attending a college course on learning theory, classroom management, or action research
- Allow ICs from other buildings in the district to come together for the day or an afternoon to share information on promising practices and effective strategies as well as challenges and barriers
- Allow ICs to purchase materials and resources essential to the further development of their own learning

USING DATA TO SUPPORT THE ILT AND IC

Data are important not only to an IC but to the entire ILT. Research has shown that schools that have made improvements in student achievement and have addressed key critical issues present in their buildings use data regularly in order to do so. Despite the fact that we are in a current data culture, where everyone is aware of the importance of data and is instrumental in collecting it, it is important to keep in mind the shift in perspective this new data-driven culture brings to the table.

Data used to be used to answer the question *how did we do?* Today, data use in schools has taken on a much different meaning, asking the questions *how are we doing?* and *what can we do to improve while we are still working?* In this light, data can be seen as much more formative in nature. In fact, using data to identify an issue that needs to be addressed and then using the same data points to monitor student progress or teacher performance no longer is something that is done at the end of process for summative purposes. Data are used throughout the entire process, guiding every step of the way. Data are used to inform what is being done as it is being done.

Many ILTs and ICs are used to working with data; however, even for the most experienced of users, it is important to keep in mind that there are different types of data found in school systems (Stiggins and Duke, 2008). Knowing these types of data and the assessments that produce such data as well as their benefits and limitations are critically important for ILTs and ICs who will be using this data for ongoing building improvement.

Perhaps one of the most common and most widely recognized types of data found in schools is what is referred to as **accountability data**. These are the data that come from high-stakes assessments. These assessments are usually developed by state and/or federal education agencies and administered to students on an annual basis. In most cases, these accountability measures are focused on certain content areas and a number of years of lower student performance on such measures could put a school building or district on a school-in-need-of-improvement list.

This summative data are useful to help guide the ILT and the ICs in identifying big areas of weakness, such as a large percentage of males not performing to benchmark on an annual state assessment. However, Stiggins and Duke (2008) and other experts note that one of the challenges with using this type of data as the only source is that it tells the practitioner very little about student learning and student comprehension. In addition, the data often comes to school districts too late, long after the students have moved to the next grade (or not) to be of any use for formative purposes. Many times, ILTs focus too heavily on this accountability data, holding multiple meetings so that members can conduct in-depth analysis of this data. In many cases, the ILT use only this type of data as their guiding light for school improvement. While these data are certainly important, in order for the ILT to fully support the intricate work of the IC, other types of data need to be examined and monitored closely.

Building-level data are another type of data that is available to the ILT. While this data does come from standardized measures (e.g., IOWA or TerraNovas), they are not data that place a school or district on a need-of-improvement list. These data are collected on students annually, either in the beginning or end of the school year, and they often are used internally to better understand how students are performing. It is important that the ILT and IC examine building-level data in the work they are doing, since many of the measures used to assess students are developed on *norm-groups*. This means that student results for your school building are not compared to other students in your building but rather are compared with students who have helped *norm* the test on a national or regional perspective. It means that a student's individual score is no longer interpreted in comparison to how he or she did in the class but against the norm group. Raw scores from these test make little sense (e.g., a raw score of 500) until you interpret through standard deviations and learn that a raw score of 500 is at the mean of the normal group. This will give members of the ILT a broader perspective of where students stand. These standardized tests can also be administered annually to track students' growth.

Classroom-level data allow the ILT and the IC to examine how individual classes are doing on the day-to-day learning that is taking place. Data that would fit into this category would include (but is not limited to) unit or chapter tests given by the teacher and analyzed across the entire classroom.

Student-level data are another type of data that should be examined by the ILT. These are formative data that are collected within the context of the classroom. These data could be collected by the teacher on a daily, weekly, or monthly timeline, depending on the purpose and what is being assessed. Often overlooked and underexamined (Stiggins and Duke, 2008), student-level data play an important role for tracking individual student progress on a day-to-day basis. For the IC, student-level data are important when working directly with the classroom teacher, because they allow a clearer window in order to closely examine how an individual student is learning as well as barriers that may be impeding that student's present and future success in the classroom. This kind of data includes weekly quizzes in science or math, student attendance, student office referrals, and student completion of homework.

School records and demographic data are another type of data that should not be ignored by the ILT. Examples of this data include (but are not limited to) student attendance records, student behavior data, and designations for free/reduced lunch, ethnicity, or general education/special education.

The last category of data that can be helpful to the ILT is **individual student self-regulator data.** These are data that are at the individual student level; these data come from each individual student, who is in charge of monitoring his or her own daily successes as well as establishing goals for areas that need to be improved. The difference between this and individual student data is that students are examining this data for themselves and determining its implications and importance for their own learning and success.

As you can see, all of these types of data should be part of the plan laid out by the ILT in determining what needs to be improved and how to monitor and assess steps toward such improvement along the way. In theory, success would not be achieved at accountability data unless all the other layers of data showed success as well. For example, it would be unusual for the majority of students to perform well on an accountability measure at the end of the year when they had not performed well in class on a daily basis nor at the classroom level or building level. But would it be an unheard-of occurrence? This in itself is an interesting question that the ILT may want to confirm when examining its own student data.

THE "WHY IS THAT?" ANALYSIS TECHNIQUE

Many educators often back away from the mere mention of data, because they associate the word *data* with statistics, a course that many didn't enjoy in college. While educational researchers do conduct quantitative statistical analysis on school data, that doesn't mean that this level of analysis has to be conducted by the ILT. When working with and analyzing school data, all team members need to ask of the data is *why?* While this analysis technique sounds too simplistic to be of any value, what it does is open a door for conversation, a fresh perspective, and a realization that these data are, again, not the end point but just the beginning.

Let's take a moment and examine the following example of how this technique can be used. An ILT assembles over the summer to examine student performance on a state assessment. The team begins by reviewing how each grade level did on the assessment and through this investigation discovers that approximately 30 percent of seventh graders did not meet the state's performance benchmarks. At this point, team members apply the *why* analysis and ask, "Why is this? Why did 30 percent of the seventh graders in this one building not pass the state assessment?"

After asking *why*, team members begin to speculate and have a conversation around the data. Team members begin to express their ideas and hypotheses for why the seventh graders' data look the way that they do. This conversation brings about a host of possible scenarios and ideas that need to be further examined. Someone should be keeping track of these ideas, and the ILT should investigate them further. For example, someone on the team might want to see what teachers these seventh graders had for this content area; others might want to see the listing of students names who did not meet benchmark and want to link school record data (e.g. attendance and behavior data) with student performance on the assessment.

Did these students not meet benchmark because, as a group, they missed an unusual number of school days? If so, all the improvements in the world to classroom instruction aren't going to matter unless the ILT finds a way to get these students to attend class. All of these ideas and subanalyses begin when we ask the all-important question: *Why?*

Getting Data into the Hands of the People

If you want people to get excited about (and use) data to improve their practice, you have to make the data real to them. And you have to get them to see a purpose of the data and the data analysis. Basically, you have to get the data in their hands, and that doesn't necessarily mean giving them the data on a piece of paper. I like to have them get involved in some of the manipulation of the data. For example, I was working with a group of elementary teachers, and we were analyzing student fluency data. Each week, teachers would take time out of their busy schedule to assess student fluency by measuring the correction words per minute (CWPM) students were able to do by timing the students as they read passages. These particular groups of teachers were not exactly interested in working with me nor were they interested in analyzing their students' data. So I started our first session together by going around the circle and having each one talk about how they use the data they collected weekly on students. What I discovered was that they did very little with the actual data once they had collected it. For the most part, teachers felt as though they were collecting the data for their principal and saw very little relationship to their instruction.

The next time we got together, I had the teachers bring their data from their students for the past 20 weeks. I also brought graph paper and we began to graph student fluency data individually for each student. Afterward, we began to look for themes or patterns among the students. For example, on Week 6, many students dropped dramatically on their CWPM. Ironically, these same students also had similar drops on Week 13 and again on Week 18. I then asked the questions: Why is this? What do you think is causing these fluctuations? We went around the room again, and teachers discussed their hypotheses. Most of teachers' explanations had to do with issues other than instruction. For example, teachers said that at Week 13, students were leaving for holiday vacation and that their minds weren't on school or learning. The teachers had a similar excuse for Week 18. Looking at the large number of students who had the same dip in CWPM on those particular weeks in question, I knew there had to be more to it than holiday vacations. I know students are very excited about holidays, but not all students suddenly stop thinking or caring about school because of an upcoming holiday. There had to be more to the situation than what was being presented by the teachers in our discussion.

I then asked the teachers what the assessments were like on Weeks 13 and 18 and asked them to bring in the actual reading the students did on those weeks. Teachers brought in the readings and upon examining this, things began to get a little clearer. Both of the readings were from *reader's theatre,* which is where the student is given a section out of a play to read in order to measure fluency; however, unlike a narrative, the student has to read this section exactly how it appears on paper, stating each name of the characters in the play for every line. When we began to discuss this and how this might play into students' lower performance levels that we were seeing in the data, teachers noted that students were uncomfortable with reader's theater and didn't get a lot of time to practice with reading plays. This provided a more grounded explanation for why students were not making gains at these weeks. This new examination of the data now provided the teachers with information that could be useful to their instruction. They decided that in the future, they would work more with their students on reading plays in the classroom.

WAYS THE PRINCIPAL CAN SUPPORT THE IC

In order for the IC to be effective, both the IC and the building principal have to work well together. As you read in earlier journal entries, the relationship between the building principal and the IC is critical to the overall success of the mission and the future success of the students who work and learn in the building. Communication, collaboration, trust, and support are all key ingredients that need to be present in developing a healthy relationship between the principal and the IC and for the efforts to prosper.

HOW TO WORK WITH THE PRINCIPAL

The ability for members of the ILT—particularly the building principal and the IC—to clearly communicate and work together is critical. Recognizing that all members of the group are extremely busy, the IC may have to take it upon him- or herself to make sure that the lines of communication are also open and present. While the principal and IC will certainly get together during scheduled ILT meetings, it is also important that they communicate on a weekly basis as well. Therefore, the IC and principal should establish a set weekly time when they get together. Depending on the situation, the IC may find it helpful to have two short meetings with the principal each week: one in the beginning of the week to focus on where to head and another at the end of the week to summarize and reflect on what worked, what didn't work, and what they need to adjust for the following week.

As an IC, I found it very helpful to establish a weekly meeting with my building principal. We would set this meeting for Monday morning at 8:30 a.m. We originally tried to hold the meeting in the principal's office but soon found out that that was virtually impossible. Phone calls, . . . [teachers walking] in without appointments, unexpected parent meetings, and students being sent down all became distractions that interfered with what we were trying to do. Although we originally blocked off 45 minutes, we found that after a while, we only needed about 20 minutes to meet, go over the goals we had set for the previous week, [look at] what we had accomplished, and [find out] where we still needed to go for the week that lay ahead. We found this to be an effective method. We also found that keeping notes of our meetings and writing down what our goals and activities were kept us much more on track and created much more efficient meetings for us. Plus, it always gave us a starting point. My principal and I also found it useful to set up our weekly meeting at the beginning of the week so that we could focus on the whole week for where it was we wanted to go. We also found it very important not to cancel a meeting. In the entire school year, we only had to reschedule two meetings, both due to snow days. There were a couple of times when the principal was out of the building [during] our meeting time, and we still talked through Skype at our designated time. I found that making this meeting time a priority and following through gave an increased importance to the work that we were doing, and certainly showed me that my principal valued the work I was doing as an IC. (Interview with an IC)

DOS AND *DON'TS* FOR THE PRINCIPAL/IC MEETING

- Set a weekly meeting time for the IC and principal to get together. The purpose of the principal/IC meeting is to extend and support the goals and activities set forth by the ILT.

- Try to establish a day, time, and location for the weekly meeting.
- Try your hardest not to cancel. If you do cancel, make sure to reschedule for later on in the same week.
- It's probably best not to use the principal's office—too many distractions.
- Someone needs to take detailed notes about the meeting. Notes will allow both the principal and the IC to start the meeting by referring back to the previous week's notes, reminding themselves what was discussed and what were the goals and activities that they had decided to move forward.

SUMMARY

The instructional coaching position is an important one that offers great potential for significant academic improvement. It is a position that does not exist in isolation but rather as an integral part of the ILT. A position so new and nontraditional and demanding requires a great deal of support. It is also a position that offers support to all the other members of the team. The first order of business after the introductory plan is developed is to ensure that a system of support is in place and that all team members stand ready to provide whatever is needed.

Once that support system is in place, the IC can begin the important work that all members of the ILT have agreed upon. As the process begins, the IC must take an inventory of his or her own skills, resources, and talents. Additionally, the IC must start to visit classrooms where welcomed and to find ways to be welcomed where the metaphorical and physical doors are initially closed. The IC needs to determine what resources are at hand and where to find those that are not currently available. In short, the instructional coach can now begin to *coach!*

Effective instructional leadership requires many skills. Coaches must be leaders, followers, mentors, partners, researchers, and teammates. There are as many levels of coaching as there are members of the ILT. Coaching the willing team members is the first (and most obvious) task at hand, but there is another, more complicated layer of coaching required: coaching the reluctant. There are many reasons why teachers might be reluctant to participate in working with an IC. Reluctance could be disguising many different emotions. Those who are unwilling to join the team might, in truth, be those who are unfulfilled, discouraged, frightened, confused, or in any of a number of other states of mind. It is the IC's job to discover the reasons for this reluctance and try and try again until you reach the talented professional waiting for discovery.

Self-Study Activity #3

Conducting a *Why* Analysis with the ILT

When working with the ILT, it is important to get started right away. One of the easiest ways to get started is by conducting a *Why* analysis. Take a moment and review the methodology described above in the chapter. Although it may seem simple, you will soon find out that it can be quite powerful and informative for all ILT members. Start by having the ILT take a section of accountability data, perhaps student performance data from a recent high-stakes state assessment. Now begin by examining the data. Be sure to also separate the data and examine them more closely by key student demographics. When you have teased apart the data as far as the team can go, then ask the important question: *Why?* For example, why are 60 percent of all ESL (English as a second language) students who are also male not meeting the state benchmark on the eighth grade English Language Arts (ELA) assessment? This *why* question will naturally spark an interesting conversation by ILT members. Be sure to take detailed notes of each member's reasons for why this is happening. Then use this *why* data as a foundation for beginning the conversation amongst the team. Then the team will begin to find a program, curriculum, or intervention to put in place to address the issue at hand.

The Day-To-Day Work of the Instructional Coach

4

Mrs. Skyler Sanders, Building Principal
Journal Entry: November 1

As happens every year, the time seems to race by. I can't believe the first semester is nearly half over. As happens every year, I worry that we are running out of time to get where we need to go, but this has surely not been like every other year! Adding the instructional coach to the faculty has certainly changed the dynamics and stirred the pot. A lot has happened since the first day of school, and I believe, looking from inside the eye of the storm, that this has been a significant and positive development. For sure, we've had some roadblocks but for the school, and for me personally, the ILT has really been just what was needed.

Once we regrouped last fall and took charge of the definition of our roles as the ILT, things began to move very quickly. Once teachers understood that the instructional coach wasn't my "eyes and ears" in the classrooms, more doors were opened and the faculty seemed to find a new optimism and energy I haven't seen in years. Based on our data analysis, it was clear to all members of the ILT that a new reading curriculum was desperately needed. The focus on the implementation of the new reading series was the first key. It was a common goal and it began with everyone on a level playing field. The instructional coach also brought in help from the district at large and those partnerships are still going strong. In past years, we've had other programs brought in and they took a lot longer to take hold. Having help and resources for information right here really made the difference.

This group of new teachers seems to be assimilating much more easily and successfully into our faculty since they have the instructional coach to help answer their questions. In past years, I'd spend a lot of my time as "the evaluator" of new staff, trying to make sure they all had the information they needed on procedures, policies, and processes. I know it is hard for a new teacher to come to the principal with questions about lunch count or hall passes or home/school communication, but now they have someone to help them with all of these details; someone they see as their mentor and their coach. The instructional coach is truly their coach, helping them to work on developing their instructional skills and pointing them in the right direction for help with specific curriculum concerns or instructional practices or behavior management challenges. One teacher here is an expert in working on differentiated instructional strategies, and the instructional coach has enlisted her to help advise these "newbies." I am sure they feel more comfortable trying these new practices out with help and support. I am seeing a greater variety of approaches to instruction as I make my daily classroom walk-throughs and as I began the first round of formal observations.

We did run into a couple of problems that we had to address. The most significant was establishing everyone's role in the entire process. The instructional coach and I have worked really hard to assist the faculty to see the difference in our respective roles. However, we have to keep proving to some of the staff that the instructional coach isn't evaluating them in any way. At the same time we have to maintain control over the definition of the instructional coach's role to prevent the position from devolving into a combination substitute teacher/teaching assistant/clerical aide. While all of those roles are very real needs and all are certainly important, the instructional coach can't fall into the trap of becoming this "utility player." There just wouldn't be any time left for coaching, and coaching is what will make us better at what we do.

It started when I didn't help in defining the role and teachers began to define it for us, based on their individual needs. Once we got past that and restarted the program with a job description for the IC, things quickly got better; however, at a faculty meeting in December a small group of teachers handed me a list of needs they still had and suggested that I have the instructional coach work on these issues. They insisted the instructional coach's role be changed to include these items. I met with the IC and we talked about all of this. We decided that as coach, she would help the teachers find other resources to help fill these specific needs and to explore ways she could help fill them while still remaining focused on the coaching role, which is her primary mission. We didn't solve all the problems, but she did help one teacher to get assistance from the district reading consultant, and she helped another teacher petition for a special education Para needed in her classroom. She also did compromise a bit with one teacher, agreeing to work with a small math group as a way to model new instructional strategies and as a way into a classroom that had not previously been open to her. We felt this compromise was consistent with the IC role of developing a working partnership with all teachers. Mrs. Wright is still working with that math group, but there are plans to transition it back as part of a schoolwide project on differentiated instruction.

I also decided to move the IC's office to a small classroom in another part of the building. It gives her greater access to classrooms, provides a more appropriate conference space, and helps defend against the false premise that she is part of the administration here. I am careful not to ask her any questions that would require an evaluation of staff, and if I do stumble into that territory, have made it clear to Mrs. Wright that she should feel free to remind me that type of question is off-limits. I also stepped up my own curriculum work time schedule. I am spending more time in classrooms, communicating with staff, affirming effort, and reinforcing our strategies for success. I intervene when I have to do so based on what I personally see, hear, and know. I'll ask the coach to help with a specific problem only after the teacher in question agrees. Then, together, we meet with the IC to lay out the plan. I also call on others for assistance so the IC isn't always seen as the "fixer." That helps us to remember that coaching is everyone's role and is based on opportunity and expertise and not just on position title. I sense that the trust level is building, *but I know I have to be vigilant to make sure we don't do anything to damage the bridges that have already been built.*

I do really feel like the instructional leader of the building again. It is not perfect, and there are days I still retreat behind the curtain of my office desk, putting out fires and addressing the needs and demands that are still arriving daily. I still do have days like that, when other people and other things define my role, but I have more days when I take that proactive stance, head out into the classrooms, and provide the instructional leadership I am called upon to provide. On the days when instructional leadership is my primary focus and role, it is true that the demands of the office diminish. This is looking more and more like what I signed up for years ago.

So . . . it is midsemester. We aren't where we need to be yet—not by a long shot—but we are closer than we were yesterday and I feel like we are all moving in the same direction. We've been here before, momentarily, but we're tempted to accept progress as success. It is my job now to remind everyone that progress is progress and should rightly be acknowledged, but that success is the place we describe in our mission statement, a place we still haven't arrived at yet.

> ## Mrs. Janice Wright, Instructional Coach
> ## Journal Entry: November 1

Things have really picked up in the last few weeks. Before, when it seemed that no one was aware of what I did, I had quite a bit of free time on my hands. Now, after we collaborated and developed a job description for the position, everyone needs me. And I'll admit, it's a great feeling! Just to show how busy I am, I have decided to include a copy of my schedule. I find it very important to establish a planner each day. Even though I never have the same day twice and I often don't have the day I have planned for, I think it is important.

One of the unique aspects of being an instructional coach (IC) is that one rarely has the same day twice. While it is important for ICs to establish a daily and weekly schedule, it is also important for the IC to recognize that such a schedule may not always go as planned. Being flexible as well as practical is certainly a key to being a successful and effective IC. Presented in the box below is an example of an IC's schedule.

Instructional Coach's Planner

Monday
7:30AM: New teachers' meeting

- Presentation by Ms. Smith on differentiated instruction
- Review of learning centers strategies
- Invite teachers to individual conferences on observation process.

(Continued)

(Continued)

9AM: Grade 4 reading program project

- Check in to classrooms during reading block.
- Observe groups; collect request for help and questions for district reading coordinator.

10AM: Model lesson for Grade 3 reading program
11AM: Office time

- Call reading coordinator re: missing materials.
- Call special education director re: Ms. Jones one/one Para request.
- Send e-mail to coaches in other buildings asking for suggestion for science curriculum implementation Grade K–2.
- Prep presentation for faculty meeting on data for month of December.

1PM: Cover Grade 2 class for teacher while she observes in partner classroom—focus on math learning centers
2PM: Check on supplies requests.

- E-mail teachers with updates re: curriculum and new materials I ordered.

Tuesday
8AM: Visit classrooms with focus on learning centers. Ask for permission to share teacher ideas with faculty in weekly e-mail.
11AM: Cover Mr. Y's class so he can attend parent conference.
11:30AM: Office time

- Meet with reading coordinator for district and with Grade 4 teacher on action research project.
- Meet with Ms. Wizard (Grade 5 teacher) to plan out presentation to faculty on the new writing project.

1PM: Meetings with first-year teachers seeking advice after formal observation #2

Wednesday
7:30AM: ICs meeting at district HQ
9AM: Reading program project: District reading coach will model lesson for Grade 1. Cover other Grade 1 class so teacher can observe.
10:30AM: Classroom visits
11:30AM: Office time

- Prep work on faculty meeting presentation of December data
- Action research project planning

1 PM: Visits to Grade 5 and 6 with district tech coordinator. Demonstrate lessons and advise on tech component of math program.
3PM: Meet with principal to review plans for faculty meeting presentations.

- Coordinate CWT schedules.

Thursday
7:30AM: Faculty meeting

- Presentation of December data and action research project with Grade 4 teachers

9AM: Office time

- Phone calls to check on special education Para request
- Prep e-mail of suggestions received from ICs re: science program K–2.

10AM: CWTs focus on K–3 reading program.

- Co-teach in Grade 2 class reading group. Collect questions for written response on reading program.

Noon: Office time

- Internet search for information on differentiated instruction/special ed.
- Meet with school behavior plan coordinator re: Friday rewards assembly.

2PM: Class visits and advising for first and second year teachers

Friday
9AM: Help prep for behavior plan rewards assembly.
10AM: Behavior Plan rewards assembly
11AM: Meeting with university partner reps. re: action research project
1PM: CWTs
3PM: Office time

- Call reading coordinator to debrief week's progress and plan next sessions.
- E-mail idea list (with permission) from ideas observed during classroom visits this week. Ask for return reply e-mails with suggestions, questions, and ideas.

GETTING STARTED

As a new IC, one of the hardest things to do is to get started. Like a painter facing a blank canvas or a writer staring for hours at a blank computer screen, the IC will have to separate from the ILT and face the lonely walk down the corridor and pick a point in which to begin work. Some ICs find it helpful to get the lay of the land before they begin to work. This can be easily done by gathering some initial data from teachers and staff about areas they think need to be focused on in the classroom or with the current curriculum or program. This type of data collection from participants is often referred to as a *needs assessment.* If this is the route the IC decides to go down, it is important to keep in mind that one does not want to overburden teachers and staff with complex data collection methods or take up too much of their already overtaxed time.

A recommended method for collecting initial needs assessment data from teachers is the *survey.* The survey will allow the IC to collect data quickly and not require too much of the teacher's time or take away too much attention from the classroom. The basic *needs assessment survey* is interested in gathering key bits of information from teachers. Example survey questions include the following: In what areas of classroom instruction do teachers need more assistance or training? What components of the current curriculum or program are ineffective or difficult for students and could be improved upon? What areas or topics related to classroom instruction do teachers feel they are particularly good at and would be interested in sharing with others?

Since there are technical aspects of survey design and development that are too in-depth for this book, we have supplied the IC with a sample survey. This survey can serve as a guide to show ICs the proper layout of items and the scope and sequence of survey items that are effective for gathering essential needs-assessment data from teachers and staff. A copy of this survey can be found in the IC toolbox in Chapter 10.

BASIC WAYS TO WORK WITH TEACHERS

In order to be as effective as possible, the IC will want to use a wide variety of techniques and configurations when working with teachers. One such method employed by ICs is buildingwide meetings. These large meetings would include teachers and staff from the entire school. An IC would not want to overuse this type of approach but would find this method beneficial for a day or half-day overview of a new reading, math, or science curriculum the building or district was going to be implementing in the next several months or next school year. Another configuration that the IC can employ is working with small groups of teachers. These small groups can be done at a specific level, and focusing on these small groups would provide the IC with opportunity to give an overview of the new curriculum or program to all teachers, so everyone was starting on the same page. In this case, the IC might decide to break up the larger group into small working groups during the day. These smaller groups would allow for more focused learning. In such a case, the IC may decide to have the smaller breakout groups be grade-level groups.

Another method that the IC will most likely employ is working individually with teachers. These one-to-one sessions provide the most direct application when working with the IC and provide the IC with much more ability to provide just-in-time instruction to teachers. During one-to-one sessions, the IC will most likely visit the classroom and provide a combination of modeling, observation, and feedback.

WORKING WITH TEACHERS IN THEIR CLASSROOMS

While it may appear simple, working with a teacher in his or her classroom is a challenge for an IC, even when the teacher is willing and motivated to have the IC present. When working with the teacher in the classroom, it is important that the IC keep a few key components in mind:

Keep initial visits short, simple, and to the point. Because time is of the essence, make sure that as the IC, you don't wear out your welcome the first time you go to a teacher's room. A natural reaction by many ICs is to block out a chunk of time with the teacher and provide an overview of everything that the IC has to offer. While this may seem like a good strategy to use, in fact it may suggest the wrong idea to the teacher: "This is going to take a lot of my time, time when I need to be teaching my students." In fact, the effective IC wants to do just the opposite on the first visit to the classroom.

During this short first visit, the IC should focus on just one idea to share with the teacher. This might be an instructional strategy that the IC is modeling for the week.

Teach and leave. As the IC, you also want to convey to others that your time is important. So after modeling the lesson, be sure to thank the teacher and leave. Hanging around the classroom for the next hour to observe will only create more uneasiness with the teacher. It will also convey the idea to the teacher that you have nothing else to do. Think of it as inviting someone over for a cup of coffee, and ending up with them spending the whole day and staying on for dinner. With someone like this, you are more likely to think twice about inviting the person back, knowing that the person is going to want more of your time than what you are willing to give. The same holds true for wearing out your welcome in a classroom you are visiting.

Highlight talent in the building. As the IC, it is important to recognize that there is talent all over the building. Even the most resistant, negative teacher has expertise in content, teaching, and learning. Recognizing this, and that the building could benefit from this expertise greatly, the IC should try to gather information about *who is good at what.* This could be particularly important information when setting up in-house professional development sessions with teachers or simply if the IC needed some assistance from experts in the building.

Bring teachers together. Do not always think that the IC has to be the one doing the modeling. The IC can also serve as a just-in-time substitute teacher so that two teachers who want to work together and share practices can do so. The IC can cover one of the teacher's classes for a period so that the teacher can go in and model her success practice for her colleague across the hall. Even in cases where the IC could have gone in and modeled the practice, strategically it is more valuable to have colleagues see the IC in a role other than the disseminator of knowledge in the building.

Come prepared with instructional materials. When going to the classroom to model a lesson or instructional strategy, it is important that the IC have all the materials he or she needs to do the lesson. It is also important that if there are materials involved that the IC has enough of them to go around, so every student receives one and is able to work appropriately in the classroom. Relying on the classroom teacher to create more materials in order to further implement the strategy after the IC leaves the classroom will most likely result in the teacher not executing the strategy again.

Explain your position there. As the IC, even though you know why you are in the classroom, the teacher may not. In many cases, the teacher has forgotten exactly why. Be sure upon entering the room that you remind the teacher once again what your purpose is, what you will be working on specifically today, how long you will be there, and when and how you will conduct a follow-up. This way, the teacher will not be worrying about what you are doing and can focus on the work at hand—improving classroom instruction.

SUMMARY

The job of an IC is not one that is idle or stagnant. Each day brings new things to do and new challenges that stand in the way of getting things done. For the new IC, knowing where to get started can pose one of the biggest challenges. The IC should not feel alone or work alone. The IC is an extension of the ILT and should be supported by the ILT in all the activities and endeavors relating to improving classroom instruction. One of the first steps the IC should take is to get an understanding of what area of the building needs the most work. One of the best ways to do this is to involve teachers and staff in this process and use a survey. The survey would be used to collect initial information from teachers about what they would like assistance with. From there, the IC can begin to divide up teachers into small groups by either content or grade level and work with these groups to get a more in-depth understanding about where the gaps in instruction lie. Then the IC will use a variety of techniques to work with teachers, go into classrooms, observe, and model best practices.

Self-Study Activity #4

Instructional Coach Information Questionnaire

Sometimes there is so much that needs to be addressed that it is difficult to pick a spot to begin. Instead of having the instructional coach decide where to begin first, take a slightly different approach and ask the school community what they believe needs to be improved. It is important to make sure that, as the instructional coach, you narrow the conversation to improving classroom instruction and increased student achievement. Here is a short questionnaire that an IC can use to gather information on what teachers want to work on. In the beginning, an IC might want to collect such information from teachers using an anonymous question- naire. This will provide the IC with general information on what teachers want to work on. It will not be able to give specific needs for a specific teacher. Once the IC has worked with teachers and developed a relation- ship, the IC can decide to have teachers provide their names in order to give specific assistance. Data collected from this questionnaire can also be shared and discussed with a building's instructional leadership team.

Instructional Coach Information Questionnaire

Name: (optional) _____

Grade level: _____

Building: _____

What are some topics/issues that you would like more information about?

_____

_____

_____

_____

_____

How would you best be served by this information? Check off all that apply.

_____ Written form (a book, research article, etc.)

_____ DVD

_____ Web-based video

_____ Modeling by someone else

_____ Discussion groups

_____ Formal professional development

_____ Embedded professional development

_____ Other (please explain) _____

What are areas in your classroom that you would like assistance with?

_____

_____

_____

_____

_____

When is the best time to talk about how we can arrange for me to come into your classroom? _____

Many times, we know of methods our colleagues use but never have the time to observe them or learn more about what they do. If there is a particular teacher that you would like to observe during your class time, I can take your class so that you can do so.

What is the name of the teacher you would like to observe? _____

Grade level: _____

Time of day or period: _____

Specific content or method you would like to observe: _____

An Idea for the Day 5

*Strategies and Ideas to Encourage
Engagement Between Teachers
and the ILT*

**Mrs. Janice Wright, Instructional Coach
Journal Entry: November 12**

Wow, my days are so busy now, I can hardly breathe! My schedule is full, and I'm finding that more and more of the faculty have embraced this whole concept of instructional coaching. With fewer and fewer exceptions, I've been welcomed into classrooms and been invited to offer advice, assistance, and collaboration in ways that feel right to me, given the mission at hand and the purpose of this new role.

I have lots of ideas on how to expand the coaching and evidence-gathering components to include more of the teachers as true coaches. For example, I am thinking of approaching some of our teachers who have tremendous skills in working with classroom management and asking if they wouldn't mind being paired with one of the new teachers. I'm thinking maybe they could touch base with them once a day, briefly, and answer questions; nothing formal, just conversation over lunch in the faculty room, perhaps. If they are willing, maybe I could even find some coverage so new teachers could observe in their partner's classroom. Don't know how that will all work out, but it's another new idea I got from a conversation with one of the other ICs. I also thought that one of the first-year teachers has a lot of information on the use of technology in the classroom—more than anybody I am aware of on the staff. I'm going to ask her if she would be willing to do a brief presentation at the next faculty meeting on the topic. I already ran the idea by Mrs. Sanders and she loved it.

I'm getting ideas from everywhere as I flesh out the dimensions of this position: ideas from teachers, administrators, other ICs, and district personnel; from my own professional development classes; and from my professional reading (when I get a chance to do some). I wrote down these ideas to fall back on when things seem to be headed away from what I know instructional coaching should be; these are ideas to help all of us to look at teaching and learning in new ways, to reflect, to collect evidence, and to collaborate effectively.

I even have a list of all of these that I use as my "Idea of the Day." I read one each morning (or once a week, if things are just too hectic) and try to incorporate it into my schedule somehow. I've shared the ideas with the ILT, hoping to make sure our team accomplishes all that we set out to do. It helps me to be a more effective coach and an active learner! Keeps things from becoming routine, that's for sure!

Mrs. Skyler Sanders, School Principal
Journal Entry: November 12

Janice, my IC, shared with me a list of coaching ideas she's compiling. She also shared it with the whole ILT. I was impressed by how extensive the list is already. I can really see how this whole concept of instructional leadership can expand in all kinds of directions and include ideas that would never have occurred to any of us until we started looking at this process with new eyes.

I took the list back to my office along with my other papers and notes. In a quiet moment later that day, I started to reread the list. It occurred to me that with a little adjustment, this list could be my list too. When I head out every day to visit classrooms or when I plan faculty meetings or professional development sessions, I can keep one of these ideas in mind as my primary focus. My role in instructional leadership can take me in many different directions beyond my traditional approach, allowing me to coach in new ways, collect evidence I never considered before, and collaborate with my teachers on projects and professional development that will have a much more immediate and effective impact on our progress. It will keep my instructional leadership approach from retreating into old patterns, keep it from going stale. Changing the focus once in a while will help me to break out of my routine and get involved again for all the reasons I got into this job in the first place.

And, I can start my own list of ideas to pursue and to share. Actually, I think that might just be my first "Idea of the Day!"

Mrs. Karin Hill, Veteran Teacher
Journal Entry: November 12

Had a conversation with our instructional coach today. Janice had a great idea to share. She suggested I set aside a notebook to record progress, successes, and reasons for celebration. She asked if I would leave this notebook out on my desk so that she and Mrs. Sanders could look at it when they visit my room. I didn't know what to think at first. Feels a little like bragging, but then I thought about all the times I wished someone would affirm what my students and I are doing in here and I thought, why not? So, I'm going to do it. It will help in all this evidence collection we're all involved with now, and it will be great when I get ready to write my annual evaluation review at the end of the year. By June, I am lucky if I can remember one-tenth of all that we've accomplished in here during the year, so it will be great to have that as a reference.

I've also decided I'm going to have my students keep success journals. It will be great to get them to focus more on what they accomplish and to have a visible reminder of their progress. Maybe they can use it to record growth in test results, too. I'll have them keep the journals out for parents to look at on Back-to-School night and then send them home at midyear and again in June, along with our progress reports. So often, we talk with parents about problems; I'm sure they would love to read something dedicated to their child's success.

I really like this idea. Maybe I'll share my idea for the students' success journals at the next faculty meeting when they ask about what evidence we are all collecting. Honestly I didn't know what to mention until now! We'll see. . . .

Once the instructional coach (IC) has gotten started, it is important to be responsive to the momentum that one has established by working effectively with the teachers and staff. It is also important to keep coming up with fresh ideas. These ideas not only create interest when working in a building but also provide an opportunity for the IC to build a strong bond between the instructional leadership team (ILT) and school staff. Since the IC might not be able to generate new ideas initially, we thought it would be effective to provide him or her with some ideas that were generated through our work with ICs. We call them "ideas of the day." Use them. Modify them. Add to them, and enjoy.

Idea #1: Designate a place where teachers may leave questions for the IC. As you do your walkthroughs, you might respond right away where appropriate or take the question back to your office for a written response by day's end. The sooner questions are asked and answered, the better the level of effective communication in your school. It is also the perfect way to eliminate misinformation and to quell baseless rumors.

Idea #2: If your school doesn't yet have a business partnership, think about the connections you might have via parents, faculty spouses, and so on. Many people and businesses want to help our schools but don't know exactly how they might proceed. Sometimes a simple conversation and a few well-placed suggestions can lead to a great partnership. There is money out there, and if it doesn't go to your students, it will go somewhere else. The same is true for volunteer and community organizations that might just be waiting for an invitation to partner up with your school. As always, you should check with your central office before proceeding into any type of agreement with a business or organization.

Idea #3: Divide your classroom visit notebooks into categories: teaching strategies, curriculum, classroom management, building goals, and so on. Then you can record your thoughts by category for easier reference later on. Note interesting and new data sources you uncover during your visits.

Idea #4: Don't forget that a very important component of successful instructional coaching is the ability to listen reflectively. People want to be heard. When you ask questions, give your full attention to the responses, even if there are distractions competing for your focus. It is also important to listen to what is *not* said. There is much information in what someone chooses not to say. Don't forget that some teachers, especially our newest ones, often don't ask questions because they are not sure what questions they need answers for. Good listening includes good questioning. Keep asking questions and validate efforts to respond.

Idea #5: Send out a question as part of your weekly faculty e-mail. It should be a question that is easily answered and that relates to the goals you have set as a faculty. Collect the responses for use in the next faculty meeting discussion on the issues at hand. This helps make all faculty active participants in your action research initiatives.

Idea #6: Let teachers know in advance what the theme will be for the faculty meeting discussion. Ask them to bring any relevant information/ data. Set aside the first half of the meeting for the planned discussion, and make sure each person has the opportunity to participate. Also ask para- professionals and other school support staff for any ideas and/or informa- tion they might have about the topic under discussion.

Idea #7: Ask for a spot on the faculty meeting agenda to talk about some issue related to effective teacher strategies and/or school goals. The IC could also use this time to ask a teacher to present on something discovered during the class visits or to lead a discussion on an action research project.

Idea #8: Help to establish "tag team" professional development. Coaches help teachers working on a similar challenge to form teams and work together on the issue. Another version could pair a teacher accomplished in a specific area with someone seeking assistance. Coaches and principals can make these pairings happen based on information gathered during class visits.

Idea #9: Ask an e-mail question at the end of each week that requires a one or two sentence response. Make sure it is relevant to your school's goals, compile the responses anonymously, and share with all faculty. Invite your staff to stop in to see you each day for an update on how things are going in their rooms. This ensures some face-to-face communication with every teacher, even on days that make it difficult to get into every classroom.

Idea #10: At a faculty meeting, outline two or three small challenges that plague your school; things that are perennial annoyances. Divide the faculty into two or three groups and give them the time and the authority to come up with a solution to each of these problems. Make sure that the solutions determined are implemented. At the end of the faculty meeting, people will feel like something has been accomplished, and they will be empowered. You will have two or three fewer challenges to deal with so you can focus on the bigger issues. Everyone wins!

Idea #11: Schoolwide professional development days can be great opportunities to work on data-driven decision-making projects. Encourage your faculty members to collect data for discussion on the theme of your next professional development day. Decide at a faculty meeting what data is relevant and give teachers ample time for data collection prior to the schoolwide day.

Idea #12: Principals and instructional coaches might consider spending a morning shadowing one of their most-admired colleagues. Your best advisers are your peers. Plan for a morning when you could visit another school and have a conversation with your colleague as you see what they have going on in their school. Collect ideas and solutions and build on partnerships and teams. Reinforce the idea that you are not alone in your struggles, your efforts, and your achievements.

Idea #13: At your next faculty meeting, describe an effective lesson you saw at some point recently. Have a discussion that dissects the lesson and lists the effective teaching strategies contained within it. At the end of the discussion, ask for a volunteer to present another example of a successful, effective lesson at the next faculty meeting. Make this a routine part of each future meeting, recruiting a different presenter each time. This will naturally increase the cadre of coaches on your faculty and build the instructional leadership team.

Idea #14: Often, a school might need something that is not being used at another school. Develop an e-mail "supply store" framework, where coaches can e-mail each other about specific needed items. This would save time and allow you to focus school funds on other items not readily available elsewhere.

Idea #15: "Turn and Talk" is a great classroom strategy. It is a technique used in teaching to involve students more actively in the lesson. At different points in the lessons, the students (in this case, the teachers) are asked to turn to their most immediate neighbor for discussion. The discussions are guided by specific questions to respond to, concepts to restate or expand, ideas to develop, and so on. These can be planned or unplanned if a "turn and talk" moment presents itself. Often, the teams of two or three are asked to summarize their discussions for the group (to share their ideas, ask questions they discovered in their conversation, etc.). This "report back" doesn't always need to follow. It might work as well at faculty meetings to promote meaningful discussions with the fullest participation possible. This is one activity that would help teachers to find ways to coach each other and to learn from colleagues in an informal setting.

Idea #16: Encourage teachers to list successes they wish to celebrate in a notebook left on their desks for you to view as you make your daily classroom visits. These can be moments of success, victories large and small, positive gains noted, and so on. There are all kinds of opportunities to celebrate successes that often go unnoticed and invalidated. This would help instructional leaders to acknowledge these achievements and would help teachers find new ways to collect data they otherwise might not recognize as such.

Idea #17: Use any reason to make additional walkthroughs. Delivering paychecks, dispensing long-awaited supplies, delivering messages that would otherwise be in mailboxes, and collecting responses to surveys are all good and legitimate reasons to visit classrooms.

Idea #18: Paraprofessionals are a wonderful window on the perceptions of the parents and community. You might consider handing out a brief survey that asks Paras about their perceptions of school progress and other issues. Compile a list of their insights anonymously and share it with faculty for discussion at a future meeting. This might happen several times a year to bring the paraprofessionals onto the ILT as full partners in a way that is safe and informative. This is yet another valuable source of data.

Idea #19: Hold your faculty meetings in different classrooms, so teachers can see evidence of the efforts of their colleagues. You might ask the host teacher to present on some project/action research effort in his or her classroom when you meet there. As teachers look around at their colleagues' classrooms, they can get lots of ideas, make professional comparisons, and perhaps spark a new interest.

Idea #20: Principals and instructional coaches can't get so busy that they never set aside time to talk with each other about the big ideas and beliefs about education. They must have conversations with each other about effective practice. A leadership team must always find time to know each other better and to make sure they are all on the same page (or at least in the same chapter in the same book).

Idea #21: Include in your daily announcements (hopefully via e-mail) the *focus of the day* (or week or month), which could be a vocabulary word, a test-taking strategy, or some specific component of a program that is schoolwide in scope. Highlighting one idea at a time could encourage teachers to find a way to include that focus in their plans for the day. You could talk together at the next faculty meeting and have everyone share their ideas on the focus.

Idea #22: Consider spending a half day visiting another IC for some professional dialogue and to see what is happening at another school. This is a great way to double your inventory of ideas and strategies. It also expands the circle of professional partners for you and your respective faculties.

Idea #23: A possible theme for a faculty meeting: a potluck of ideas about something your faculty is focused on. Ask each member of your instructional leadership team, including paraprofessionals and support staff, to provide one idea on the topic, either in written or verbal form. Discuss the ideas and implement those you all agree are possible solutions.

Idea #24: At your next Parent-Teacher Organization (PTO) meeting or holiday concert, give out a brief survey for parents to fill out. Ask questions that are easy to answer and collect the responses before everyone leaves. Questions could include (1) *Three things I really like about this school are . . .* ; (2) *One thing I wish I could change about our school is . . .* ; or (3) *My greatest hope for my child this year in school is. . . .* The responses to these questions, anonymously, could be a wonderful discussion topic for several faculty meetings. (See Chapter 10 for a copy of this survey.) Suggestions for change could be considered. Items discussed and changes made as a result should be reported in parent newsletters and on the agenda for the next PTO meeting. This process expands the instructional leadership team and turns parents into active researchers as well.

Idea #25: Every few weeks, e-mail your faculty with two or three questions directly related to schoolwide goals. Compile the responses, anonymously, and send out an e-mail to all members of the instructional leadership team for contemplation and for discussion at the next faculty meeting.

Idea #26: At midyear, review any and all signs of progress, plan discussion agenda items for the next several meetings, and seek volunteer discussion leaders. Review the school's mission, action research plans, and progress on goals. Refocus everyone back on the mission and celebrate progress.

Idea #27: Always end each day and each week with some positive data that reflects progress on goals.

Idea #28: Turn students into active researchers. Hold grade-level meetings that focus on data. In a simplified presentation, have the students look at school results and their progress as a grade in past years. Bring students into the discussion as members of the instructional leadership team in ways that help them take ownership.

Idea #29: Focus on data sources for discussions on special education issues and inclusive classrooms. Encourage teachers to look at individualized education programs (IEPs) as data sources as well as mandates.

Idea #30: In your daily e-mails to faculty, offer some generalized insights based on classroom walkthroughs. It would be good to note positive developments observed as well as requests for advice and suggestions as they relate to concerns you might have. These should, of course, be based on program and climate, not on individual teacher performance. These insights could be coupled with a request for some supporting or relevant data for use in faculty discussions on these issues.

Idea #31: Before your next faculty meeting, e-mail everyone and ask them to send you a list of three things they are proud to have accomplished during the school year thus far. Reproduce these items as a general and anonymous list to be read and celebrated at the meeting.

Idea #32: Ask students how they feel they are progressing and what thoughts they have relating to their school. A short survey, given in each classroom with responses collected for review by faculty, might be one way to solicit relevant data from students. Another might be a school-wide project seeking student ideas, concerns, and views in ways that are empowering to the students. The students' voice must be heard as part of the instructional leadership team.

Idea #33: Periodically ask teachers to e-mail suggestions for discussion topics and make sure to use some of them at meetings. As always, notify everyone of the discussion topic in advance and ask them to collect any and all relevant data to be considered as part of the conversation.

Idea #34: An important question to ask at every instructional leadership team meeting is *how can we take the successes we have achieved thus far and apply them to the next week, the next month, and the next year under potentially different circumstances?*

Idea #35: In your daily communication with faculty, focus on a new source of data that would not fit into the traditional ideas of what data really is. Examples include data collected at the classroom or building level and should be relevant to discussions you are currently engaged in as a school instructional leadership team. Accept any and all ideas for new sources of data as suggested by faculty, staff, students, and parents. Visible displays of data collection are visible statements that the school is always looking to improve.

Idea #36: How about a materials swap during a faculty meeting? Have teachers bring materials they are no longer using and are willing to share with other teachers.

Idea #37: Is there a data collection project that needs to be undertaken? Is there a group of students that needs a challenge? How about putting some students in charge of the collection (where appropriate) and having them present the data to the rest of the instructional leadership team?

Idea #38: Instructional leadership teams need to schedule time to meet. Much of the work happens organically, but without specifically scheduled meeting times, many of the opportunities for sharing, decision making, and data collection are lost or repeated unnecessarily.

Idea #39: Spend the next several opportunities you have while doing walkthroughs and/or classroom visits developing an inventory of your school's strengths. Post it, e-mail it to faculty, and share it in your school's newsletter. Celebrate these documented strengths and use them as the basis for future plans.

Idea #40: Partnerships are powerful. Why not pair up with another school in your district and form a partnership? You could combine resources on many levels: shared schoolwide professional development; multiclass projects; shared resources; partners in reflective practice, team projects, and friendly competitions; and an expanded base of participants in planning, brainstorming, and professional discussions.

Idea #41: Host a testing debriefing day for your school. Give students a chance to talk about the testing process they have experienced this year. Get their opinions on the preparation and actual test-taking processes from their perspective and collect their ideas for future efforts. Talk a bit about what this testing tells us and how it helps them. Give them a chance to voice their impressions, concerns, questions, and ideas about this very difficult process. Talk with them about the whole concept of data collection and decision making as it applies to them. Help them to own the process at some level.

Idea #42: At your next parent meeting, survey the group to add to the school's inventory of strengths. Then share the list in your next newsletter.

Idea #43: Recruit faculty as volunteers to become "summer e-mail buddies" for any new faculty members you will be bringing on board and for second- and third-year teachers who will still have lots of questions and concerns. Bringing on more faculty members in the role of mentor will be a way to keep people motivated and active as members of the instructional leadership team, and it will also be a great way to introduce new teachers to the ILT as well.

SUMMARY

An effective IC is not one that has a bag of tricks but someone who is able to work with people, communicate, and never lose sight of the overall goals, purpose, and mission. It is important to keep in constant communication with teachers and staff so that they know the IC is always available and present in the building. Sending out weekly e-mails informing teachers of different strategies and promising practices is essential to sharing, learning, and building community among all those involved. It also allows the IC to *show* teachers (not just *tell* teachers) the important role that the IC can play in coordinating information and thus in making teachers' lives and jobs easier.

Remember, it is important to continually document the successes along the way. The following survey will help the IC gather promising practices and materials from teachers. These promising practices will be useful in continuing discussions and sharing among teachers in the building in order to improve classroom instruction. As the IC, it is also important that you help coordinate not only the discussions but any data or materials that may need to be present in order to facilitate these conversations and provide a deep, rich discussion.

Self-Study Activity #5

Name: _____

Date: _____

1. What was one success you had in your classroom this week with a student or with the entire class? Describe the situation and how you did this.

_____

_____

_____

_____

_____

Would you be willing to share this practice and/or material with other teachers? ___ Yes ___ No

2. How can you take the successes you described above and apply them to the next week, month, or year under potentially different circumstances?

_____

_____

_____

_____

_____

3. What discussion topics are you interested in talking about at the next meeting?

_____

_____

_____

4. Are there any data/materials/resources/information that we will need to have present at the meeting to further the discussion and conversation? ___ Yes ___ No

If yes, please specify:

_____

_____

_____

Assessing Individual and Group Strengths

6

Strategies for Working With the Resistant Teacher

Mrs. Judy Thomas, Veteran Teacher
Journal Entry: November 14

Another year to get through. It's my twentieth year here, and all I want to do is to just keep my head down and get through it. I'm a good teacher. I do the best I can, but things are different! I had some new ideas for projects this year, like always, but frankly, I just don't have the emotional energy to do something new. After the last set of test scores came back for our school, it seems like I'll have all I can handle just focusing on them. Besides, I do reach a lot of the students, and my kids are pretty good when they are with me in class. I think I'm doing all that I can right now. I like my students; I really do. After all, it's been just me and them working together in our classroom, and I kind of like being able to fly under the radar and staying out of the fray.

So, I came to work this fall with one or two new ideas and a basic plan to keep to myself and do what works for me. I've given up that project I started with cooperative learning. It went pretty well, but it is a lot to start up each year, and no one seemed to know or care about it while I was doing it. It's just easier not to bring it up again. Then there was the year I had the kids doing interactive journaling with me and with each other as part of our writers' seminars. It was great, and I loved writing with them. The book we published was really special. The kids and their parents loved them. I thought it was great, but no one else here seemed to think so. I never heard much about it, so by the next year I thought, why bother? I do miss the program I was part of when I first transferred to this school. The writing/art/ reading integrated unit we did every year on the Roman Empire for social studies was awesome. When the reading teacher got involved, it just seemed to really take off. The kids did very well and loved it too. Two years later, the art teacher transferred to a middle school. The reading teacher and I did a modified version of it for a year or so, but it never really caught on as well and then her position got reduced to half-time here. It just became impossible to keep it going. I tried to find other staff to work on it with me but didn't get anywhere with that, so it's back to just me and the kids on our own. It's not that I don't want to do more, but I can't see how this can happen without some help.

I was resigned to and hopeful for another quiet year. Then I got to school and heard that Mrs. Wright was our new instructional coach. Instructional coach? What is an instructional coach? First I thought she was going to help with the standardized testing program as a coordinator or that maybe she was our adviser for the new reading series. Then the school worked together to come up with a job description for the position. Talking about putting the cart before the horse. You would have thought that they would have come up with the job description before they put someone in the position. I don't think anyone in the building really knew what the instructional coach was supposed to do until the job description was developed. Now I understand that Mrs. Wright is supposed to be coming around to our classrooms. For what? I guess I first thought that maybe this would be a good thing—I've been asking for some paraprofessional help for years but never got someone assigned to me. When she said she'd meet with each of us to start talking about this project, I made a mental list of all the things I need—mainly I thought she could help by taking over the lowest-level reading group. Actually, if she worked with them in the library, this might be a really great idea. I'd have more of chance to work with the others and it would be a quieter reading block time. I started to make a plan for that possibility, getting ready for our face-to-face and then . . . another faculty meeting, where she and the principal went over this instructional coach role in more detail. I was relieved to hear that she wasn't coming in here to observe and report. They made that pretty clear, but as they talked, the dream of help with that reading group faded in my mind. She's coming into our room to help us become more effective and to support what we are doing in the classroom. What exactly does that mean? I've been on my own as a teacher for the last twenty years, and I've done OK. I'll make it for another five or so. I'm not volunteering for this. I've had so many ideas over the years, and they all fell flat. No one helped me. Let her help the new teachers. I am going back into my room and closing the door. I don't need to get my hopes up again. I'm fine just the way things are. I know a lot of my kids could do better, but they're doing OK, and I'm just too old and too tired to change and to figure out how all this would even work. A partnership? I can't even imagine how that would work, and I just don't think I'm the partnership type.

Well, so far so good. I see Mrs. Wright is working over in C wing with the fourth grade teachers, and I see the new teachers following her everywhere like ducklings. It's great that they have someone to talk to. I remember my first year! I think back now and am amazed that I made it this far and was able to find some success pretty much on my own. Mrs. Wright is a good person and, from what I hear, a great teacher, but I'm happy the way things are. I shut my door and hang out the imaginary "Do Not Disturb" sign. I am hanging in there; the kids are working OK, and hey, only seven more weeks until winter break!

Mrs. Janice Wright, Instructional Coach
Journal Entry: November 14

There are still several teachers who just haven't invited me into their classrooms. They let me come in for a few minutes when I am going on some of my daily rounds, but that's it. They didn't ask for help, don't suggest any projects for us to work on together; they really haven't embraced the IC idea at all . . . yet! I'll be spending some time every day trying to think of ways I might be able to work with them. I'm going to do some research, formal and informal, about why they might be so resistant. I don't believe they are not good teachers. People who have been here for a long time talk sometimes about what great teachers they are (or were), and often former students show up, many of them parents of current students and seem to have fond memories of these teachers. I think it is more a case of excellence that has been allowed to hibernate behind walls of frustration and protective apathy. I have some ideas about how to get past all of that. We talked about it at our last instructional coaches' meeting, too. I just have to decide on what the best approach would be for each person and be patient! I need to build trust and develop these professional relationships very slowly. I have high hopes that our evidence-collection project focusing on the new reading program might just be the key. After all, we are all in the same boat when it comes to this new program. I'm sure these teachers have a lot to offer as coaches if I can just break down the walls a bit. I am sure going to try!

Mrs. Kirsten Blum, Teacher and ILT Member
Journal Entry: November 15

At our last meeting, we talked a bit about how to bring onboard some of the teachers who have so far shown no interest in getting involved. The IC has clearly been thinking about this and gave us some insights on the topic. Mrs. Sanders, our principal, talked about some of the facts of life that often lead to teacher frustration. She mentioned budget cuts, changing personnel, a lack of affirmation and recognition, and the traditional isolation of teachers in the past, which I remember as the "egg crate" organization—we all were in our separate rooms, working pretty much alone with little chance for collaboration.

I'm glad we had the discussion because, truthfully, I just wrote these teachers off as burned out or mediocre, but now it occurs to me that maybe under all the layers of what seems to be apathy or negativity, there probably lies a talented educator whose frustration limit was reached years ago.

The IC seems to think that our project on collecting evidence for the new reading program may be the way to build some bridges, open some doors, and help teachers to climb back out from behind these walls and agree to give it one more try. I hope so. We need everyone's help if we're going to make the significant progress we set as our goal for this year.

In the meantime, the discussion has given me a lot to think about. What, I wonder, can I do to reach out to my colleagues who seem so distant? There are people on this faculty I haven't had much to do with in years. That needs to change. These are my colleagues after all, and we are all in the same boat. Hmmm . . . lots to think about!

WHO IS THE RESISTANT TEACHER?

The story above is an example of what happens to excellence allowed to hibernate, to talent hidden in a system of bureaucratic isolation. What we have shown is an example of reversible apathy. Mrs. Thomas clearly is a teacher who stumbled a bit early in her career but who found her bearings and worked very hard to do a good job. She is someone who cares about her students and wants them to do well. She also is a person who has become what we might, at first glance, consider to be burned out. . . . But is she really?

There are a lot of clues in what she had to say here that demonstrate a desire to be innovative, to work collaboratively, and to make change. She has reached out and, for a time, has experienced some success in her attempts to change the story. Yet here she is; content to be left alone with her students and willing to accept what levels of success she believes are possible. She wants to be left alone and, in doing so, to be left behind. If that happens, all the talents, knowledge, experience, and enthusiasm still clearly present within her will be lost to her students, to her school, and to her profession.

This is a teacher that some might see as having surrendered to what she believes to be insurmountable odds; someone counting the days until the next vacation and the years until retirement. But is that really the final verdict here?

The instructional coach (IC) will find no welcome here, at least not right away. The "Do Not Disturb" sign has been posted on the teacher's door. The instructional coach just cannot leave that sign there, that door closed. The instructional coach can, in a case like this, make a difference that will change the game for the teacher, these students, future classes, and for all the colleagues this good teacher might one day coach herself. How can this happen? The instructional coach has to find the key that opens this door and then he or she must become a prospector! He or she needs to search for hidden treasure and the IC might have to make his or her own treasure map.

THE IC AND PRIVATE INVESTIGATOR

The instructional coach needs to search for clues. This teacher has a history of having done some pretty innovative things. She clearly has done well in collaborative efforts in the past. She seems to have some skills in and a passion for writing—a skill that challenges many students in our schools. This teacher demonstrates caring and concern for the new faculty and perhaps could be a coach herself for this fledgling group of educators. She also has some level of expertise in an area with which other teachers often struggle: she knows a lot about cooperative learning.

The instructional coach will not, of course, be privy to the teacher's private thoughts, but in casual conversations, clues will reveal some insights. Perhaps some small project could provide the opportunity for this teacher to get back onboard the road to excellence. The instructional coach will just have to try a few strategies until there is an open door and a hidden talent found, and then a real partnership can start to build that will bring great benefits to everyone!

There are many teachers in our schools who, intentionally or not, are keeping their talents under wraps. There are many teachers hiding in protective apathy. There are many teachers yearning to be affirmed and to have their talents rediscovered. We cannot afford to give up on any of our colleagues. The instructional coach just needs to start the search. There is treasure to be found behind every closed classroom door!

SEARCH AND RESCUE: THIRTEEN STRATEGIES FOR MINING FOR GOLD

While it is true that there are some teachers who will never really buy in to this process, we believe two things are true: First, it becomes increasingly difficult to stonewall in the face of success as more teachers participate in and benefit from the instructional coach/instructional leadership team (ILT) partnership. True resisters become more isolated, and it will be far more difficult for anyone to continue to be willfully mediocre, if that was ever really their goal. Second, most naysayers are talented and committed educators who have become discouraged and disheartened over the years. They are reluctant to get their hopes up one more time and protect themselves instead with silence, withdrawal, or the persona of cynicism. "Bah, humbug" becomes their mantra, but what they are really saying is "Not again!" Beneath that exterior of mediocrity or surrender, there is often a talented educator yearning to be successful once more. The IC cannot give up on breaking through these protective walls. There is hidden excellence waiting for discovery. It is not an easy task. These teachers have been through many new initiatives, programs, experts, and projects. They have felt the sting of failure and blame and the frustrations of struggle and have been discouraged from taking any risk. They are burrowed deep inside layers of apathy, mistrust, and fear and have embraced the status quo as the only safe harbor in the storm. They aren't burned out; they are just burned! Their talents lie hidden and unused, but they are there. There's gold in them there classrooms, and the IC must find ways to uncover it again and let it shine. Grab your pick axe, your shovel, and your gold pan, and let's head out!

1. *Tiny flakes are still gold.* Act on the smallest opportunity. Find some small way to be helpful, and leverage that into an ongoing conversation. Cover the class for a few minutes. Provide copies of a needed worksheet. The specifics do not matter; what is important is that you are seen as helpful and nonjudgmental. Use what you learn from these encounters to expand the conversation.

2. *Look for a common vein of gold.* Find a common need. Perhaps this teacher can help with some schoolwide effort. Maybe he or she has expressed a need that is similar to something the IC is working on with others. Extend an invitation to join in the work on this one specific item; you might get a "yes." Once on board for this one item, you can help build relationships that have possibly been dormant for years. Colleagues may see this teacher with new eyes.

3. *Start with a small claim.* Take small steps. Make the first contacts about very specific small tasks or projects occurring during a brief window of time. Many small steps, building on success, lead to more small steps, and maybe, just maybe, some longer walks and exciting journeys.

4. *It's the claim, not the crew.* Focus on the project and not the person. Is there a schoolwide goal that needs more data collection? Perhaps an invitation might be extended into this classroom to collect information or to observe a new program's implementation, rather than to focus on this teacher's skills. Often people are happy to help if they don't feel they might be judged in some way. The teacher might also take a more active role in the ensuing conversation about this schoolwide effort once his or her own contributions are included in the study.

5. *Follow the map.* Search for clues. The hidden treasures aren't easy to find, but there are always clues. Listen carefully in conversations with these teachers. What are they interested in or passionate about? Something they love to do might just be a bridge into their classroom or a way to invite them to help someone else. A math teacher, for example, might play in a band on weekends and therefore might be easy to involve in a project of integrated curriculum using music and algebra and art. No clues in the chatter? Then check out the history. Were there any projects in the past in which these teachers were actively involved? Did they ever supervise an afterschool program or project? Have they ever led an initiative? Perhaps something in the current plan includes a similar theme. If so, it could be a way to call on skills lying dormant; old interests could be reawakened and past efforts could become the building blocks for present efforts.

6. *Keep searching.* The "no" often contains a "yes" if you listen carefully. Hidden within the excuses, the complaints, and the refusals lie clues to the true talents and concerns and passions beneath the surface. Within each "no" is the potential key to a future "yes." All you have to do is listen to all that is said and all that isn't said. Once you find a clue, you may just have found a way to reopen the classroom door that has been closed to you until this moment. If not today, maybe tomorrow or a week from now, but surely one day soon, an invitation may arrive based on a clue you have already received.

7. *Expand the search.* An invitation to join in some schoolwide project is less threatening than a request for a one-to-one partnership to those who have spent so much of their career in a collaboration-free zone. For many teachers, a second adult presence in their classrooms has always meant judgment and evaluation. For those reluctant to embrace the IC partnership, perhaps an invitation to participate in some small way on a team event would be a safer way to enter the process. Often, all these teachers need is time to prove their suspicions wrong.

8. *Keep digging.* "No" doesn't always mean "never." Often "no" means "not now" or "not yet" or even "ask me again." Once this teacher has seen the IC in action and has heard some positive feedback from colleagues, "no" might become "maybe" and even "yes" at some future point. If you don't keep asking, the teacher may take your respectful silence as dismissal or as surrender. Find different ways to ask, but keep asking.

9. *Pair 'em up.* Perhaps this teacher has a particular colleague they feel comfortable with. Maybe your path to a relationship with Mr. Reluctant is one that leads to this colleague you have in common. You might suggest a project or task that takes three and recruit the pair to work together with you. As your team of three progresses, you'll find new ways to bring out the best in everyone involved, including you!

10. *Eliminate the fool's gold quickly.* Solve problems quickly! Sometimes the smallest problem solved for this teacher is the way to a beautiful friendship. Maybe this teacher has some minor concern or struggle you can resolve. Even if it isn't part of your IC job description, seize the moment and solve the problem. Accept, for the time being, the definition of the help he or she needs. Once you are invited into this classroom, you'll have the chance to get back on the IC/ILT track, but you'll never get this teacher on board if you pass up the chance for a first conversation.

11. *Let your crew find new gold.* Find new roles for this teacher; ones that bring his or her hidden talents to the surface once again. Has Mr. Reluctant ever been asked to be a leader? Does he have some specific knowledge base

that everyone on the faculty would benefit from learning? Is there a project that he might sign on for? Often a new role, no matter how small or finite in duration, can help give a tired teacher a new sense of energy and a belief in the possible and the probable. It can revitalize a career and bring a new and wonderful dynamic to the process. A new set of challenges may revive a career that has been languishing in isolation and low expectation.

12. *Celebrate the discoveries.* Confirm and affirm. Confirm what this teacher wants, knows, and can do. Applaud successes sincerely. Affirm the talents and accomplishments in evidence. Speak positive truths, and help find ways to uncover more light. More than anything, teachers want to be affirmed for their efforts, their successes, and their accomplishments. It costs nothing, and it can nourish a career that will inspire others for a long time to come.

13. *Share the treasure with the crew.* Once you uncover the gifts, the talents, the knowledge, the skills, and the passions hidden in these classrooms, find ways for this newly discovered gold to be shared. The treasure you find can be used to make everyone better. Success builds upon success and, as the light spreads, there won't be any more dark and forgotten corners. More gold will surely be found.

SUMMARY

The ILT should make sure that it doesn't forget the hidden talent of its teachers and staff. While it might not be initially obvious, all school buildings are filled with hidden talent waiting to be recognized. Even the most resistant teacher has talents, and it is the responsibility of the IC to systematically go about identifying such talent in the building and using it to foster model practices for other teachers. While there is no guide for the IC for working with resistant teachers, it is important for the IC to understand that there are some key components that might be useful. Finding a teacher's hidden talent, finding a new role for the teacher, pairing teachers together for modeling and sharing, communicating, celebrating, and even just being a good listener are all techniques that the IC can employ to win over and work with the resistant teacher. Once converted, the resistant teacher will become a staunch ally for the ILT.

Remember that a successful IC is one that brings people together as well as provides effective instructional strategies and practices. When trying to get teachers together, the IC can act covertly, putting two teachers together specifically so one can learn vicariously from the other (without knowing it). Here is a survey that can be used to identify talent so the IC can partner teachers up without necessarily linking effective teachers to ineffective teachers.

Self-Study Activity #6

Name: _____

Grade level: _____

School building: _____

List or describe instructional strategies that you believe you do exceptionally well.

_____

_____

_____

_____

_____

When do you do these strategies during the day?

Period: _____

Time of day: _____

Would you allow another teacher to come in and observe you teach this strategy? ___ Yes ___ No

List or describe challenges in your classroom/instruction that you would like to improve on.

_____

_____

_____

_____

_____

When is your planning period? _____

Changing Teacher Practices Through Classroom Field-Testing 7

The ILT's Role

Mrs. Janice Wright, Instructional Coach
Journal Entry: November 20

While working as an instructional coach this year, I have certainly experienced resistance. While at first I took teachers not wanting to let me into their classrooms personally, I have now come to realize that most of the resistance comes from fear: fear of the unknown and fear about what my purpose was. Establishing a job description and continually working with teachers to reinforce my purpose has certainly helped to alleviate most of the concerns that many teachers originally had; however, no matter how hard I work to establish trust and build relationships with teachers in the building, there are a handful of teachers that continue to not want my support or assistance. I have learned that I can be very successful by setting up field-testing studies in teachers' classrooms to research the effectiveness of the strategies that I am working on with them. I find that this process provides a safe framework for us to look at and research instructional practices in their classrooms. These resistant teachers are made comfortable with the fact that we are not examining their instructional practices but are testing out the practices in their room. They are more comfortable, since we are gathering data about the instructional strategy and not about them or their effectiveness as teachers. And the best part about involving the teachers in the research is that it has been a sort of covert way of getting them to engage in and see the results of the instructional practices we are trying out. I have found that once they see for themselves how effective these new instructional practices are and how students respond positively to them, they quickly and almost seamlessly incorporate them into their pedagogy. And the nice part is, I don't have to do a thing except serve as a sort of technical consultant.

I am not doing the research; I'm assisting the teachers in conducting their own field tests of strategies and interventions in their classrooms.

When I first approached teachers with the idea of field-testing strategies, I began to show them how they could begin to set up their own field-testing studies in their classrooms. This experience has also added a new dimension to our conversations at our book club and faculty meetings. Now, we also use that time to share with others the various field-testing studies that are being conducted as well as the results from those projects. In many cases, several teachers have all researched the same technique and present their findings. It is interesting to see how many times the same results will be replicated across multiple classrooms. It not only provides for a rich discussion but also shows teachers the power of conducting research in their classrooms. Who knew?

> ### Mr. Christopher Todd, Veteran Teacher
> ### Journal Entry: November 20

At first, I will have to admit, I was not interested in conducting any field-testing in my classroom. Just the name alone was enough to send shivers down my spine. I hate research. I used to think that there was no purpose for it and that the people doing all the research weren't really looking at the real issues that needed to be addressed; people with no real experience in actual classrooms with real live students! So when our building's instructional coach went to training and came back and announced that she would be working with us on projects in our classrooms, I was not interested. I went to the meeting that she had and listened, but when it came time to sign up to volunteer, I passed the sheet of paper along. I continued to attend the book club meetings, which I have found to be very beneficial. I like the level of discussion and have learned a lot. In any event, I have found the discussion about the classroom field-testing of strategies that teachers were doing to be interesting, and now I think that I, too, would like to do one. I particularly like the fact that it's not about me or my teaching; I am testing out a strategy in my classroom to see if I get the same results and come to the same conclusions as the research studies that have been used to support the research-based practice. I especially like it because it makes it (the strategy) feel as though it is really my own, since in the end, we are using the evidence from my classroom field test to make the determination whether to keep the strategy or not. Finally, research with a purpose and with a basis in the realities of a classroom! Now that is research I can see some value in!

CLASSROOM FIELD-TESTING: A POSSIBLE OPEN DOOR?

It is perfectly natural to experience some resistance (or at least anxiety) from teachers when you are going into their classrooms—even if you enter with the promise that you are going to help. As discussed throughout the earlier chapters of this book, people may have different reactions and perceptions of being helped. In any event, instructional coaches (ICs) who want to get into teachers' classrooms and assist them with improving their instruction may be quickly halted by the closing of the classroom door. This may be found more in veteran teachers who have tenure rather than new teachers who are eager to get tenure and thus eager and willing to do almost anything.

Let's say you are an instructional coach and you want to work with a particular teacher on her classroom instruction. Perhaps you know that this teacher needs some help with her classroom management skills, and even though you haven't been allowed in to observe her class, the need for some guidance in this area is apparent from the number of students that are sent to the office each period from her class. In addition, Principal Sanders has noticed this and has asked you to work with the teacher to try and address some of the issues in the classroom rather than send students down to the office.

So, how do you go about entering the room and working with this teacher on this sensitive issue? One possible approach would be to go into the teacher's classroom and ask her if you can observe her while she teaches her lesson and then give her some advice about how to better handle some of the rogue students in the class. This might be well received, but most likely it would not. Take a minute to think about how this approach might look from the teacher's point of view. What kinds of apprehension do you think the teacher might have in this situation?

One of the main problems with this approach is that it is designed to automatically put the teacher on the defensive. Again, try to image it from the teacher's perspective. The very fact that the instructional coach wants to come into her room implies that she has been doing something wrong, something that needs to be fixed. It also puts the instructional coach on a top-down leadership approach, meaning that the instructional coach has greater power than the teacher and that the instructional coach holds the correct way to manage the students and needs to disseminate this information to the teacher. In other words, one member of the party has the knowledge and is responsible for disseminating that knowledge to the other member of this dyad. If this was a street, the traffic would only be flowing one way.

Experts in leadership and professional development all agree that this type of collaborative model is ineffective for making true change. It might bring about change; the teacher might take the instructional coach's advice and respond to the rogue students when they get out of line in a different way than he or she had been responding, but in most cases, these changes in practice are not sustainable. They are done to appease someone else, and the moment that individual is out of the picture, the original practice returns.

There are many reasons why teachers fall back into old practices that are ineffective. One of the main reasons for the pedagogical lapse is because the old way just feels more comfortable; it just feels right. In addition to the other barriers mentioned above, the other obvious problem with this top-down leadership approach is that it doesn't allow for any trust to form between the two individuals (the IC and the teacher).

Instructional coaches that we worked with reported that working with a teacher—any teacher, whether they are highly receptive or resistant—can be difficult. Keep in mind that they also reported working with both new and veteran teachers who were delighted to have them in their classrooms and interested in the help that they had to provide. But there were many teachers who did not feel comfortable having instructional coaches in their classrooms. For these teachers, our instructional coaches had some success using active research as a way to open the door for communication, trust, and collaboration.

However, as discussed early in this chapter, classroom field tests can also be used as a way to open the door to teachers, both new and veteran, who may have some apprehension about having someone else in their classrooms. Let's continue with the scenario discussed earlier, the teacher who is having trouble with a few rogue students in her classroom. Let's take a look at how the instructional coach approached the teacher in the first scenario.

First scenario (I am here to help you!)

Instructional Coach: Principal Sanders and I have been looking at the office referral data for last month and noticed that you send quite a few students to the office. There are some very effective classroom management techniques that might be helpful. Maybe I can come in next week and model some of these strategies for you?

PROFESSIONAL DEVELOPMENT ACTIVITY

Take a moment to reflect on the statement above and answer the following questions.

- What are some positive aspects of the approach the instructional coach used?
- What are some negative aspects of the approach (things that may be off-putting to the teacher, even though the instructional coach doesn't mean to make them that way)?
- In your final analysis, did this approach have more positive or negative attributes?

One positive aspect of the above approach is that the instructional coach is offering assistance. She has recognized a problem or issue and is offering a possible solution: she will come in and model some classroom management strategies for the teacher. Many times in schools, issues such as this are often overlooked by administration or other colleagues. The principal and teachers know that in a particular class there are several students who have a reputation for causing trouble and too often very little is done to address the issue. With that in mind, a teacher who is at the end of his abilities in dealing with these students, who dreads every morning that he steps into the building, might just rejoice at such an offer for assistance.

On the other hand, this approach has some underlying issues. An obvious one is that from the very beginning, the instructional coach (again, without meaning to) has set a stage of two against one. By mentioning the principal, the instructional coach has already conveyed to the teacher that she or he is being watched and that some discussion or possibly even a meeting has occurred behind closed doors to discuss the issue at hand. If the instructional coach did not mention the principal, the other underlying issue with this approach is the fact that the instructional coach recognizes the problem and wants to come in and fix the teacher. According to leadership theory, this top-down approach may result in some peripheral change, meaning the teacher lets the instructional coach come in to her classroom and model the strategies in an attempt to get it over with; however, once the instructional coach moves on, the teacher is unlikely to adopt these new classroom management techniques, no matter how successful they were when the instructional coach used them to deal with the rogue students.

Now let's examine the same situation, but this time using the classroom field-testing approach: The IC meets with a small group of teachers. Included in the group is the one teacher that has the high number of students being sent to the office. In this small group, the instructional coach leads a discussion about classroom management and issues with students misbehaving in the class. Teachers begin to chime in with testimonials about what they are seeing in their classrooms, how they are trying to handle it, what seems to be working, and what doesn't seem to work. After a conversation, the instructional coach discusses a classroom management technique that she has recently learned about through reading a research-based study or attending a conference. She describes the technique to the teachers and then discusses how they could all conduct classroom field tests using the technique in their classroom to determine if the technique is effective or not. If it is effective, then they can present it to the entire staff and make it a schoolwide effort. If not, they continue to search for other behavioral techniques until they find one that works for them. The teachers agree and the instructional coach works with the group and each teacher independently to conduct an action research study. With the instructional coach guiding the process, the group develops a plan for implementing the technique and collecting data to determine if it is effective for reducing the number of incidents in the classroom and thus reducing the number of students that are routinely sent to the principal's office. Figure 7.1 is an overview of the classroom field-testing project the teachers and the instructional coach developed.

Let's take a moment to examine the research process they collectively decided upon. As part of the first data collection procedures, *baseline data* were collected. Baseline data are initial data that are collected to get an accurate reading on the situation. In other words, it is a place to start. In this case, the first questions that needed to be answered were (1) *what is the average number of in-class disturbances the targeted students exhibited in a given class period?* and (2) *what exactly are these disturbances (e.g., calling out without raising hand, disturbing the student in front of them, etc.)?* In order to establish the baseline data for these students, the teachers kept track of this information for three school days.

One of the critical aspects of conducting this type of study is that the baseline data have to be accurate or reliable. One of the teachers might come up with an average of 12 disturbances for the targeted students per class period, but is that accurate? A teacher could very easily be biased by the situation and, having had trouble with a particular student in the class before, be a bit overzealous in counting the number of disturbances. How could this affect the field testing? Later, after the techniques have been implemented, if the teacher returns to accurately counting the number of in-class disturbances, we won't know for sure if the dramatic decrease is because the new techniques are really working or if the decrease is due to the shift back to accurately tabulating the disturbances by the targeted students.

Figure 7.1   Action Research Borrows Methods From Applied Research

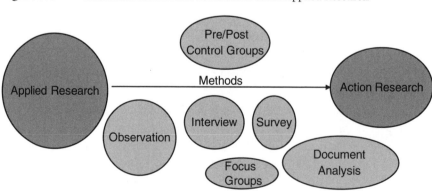

Now, here is where the instructional coach comes into the process! When using observation as a method for collecting data, professional researchers try to establish what is called *inter-rater reliability* (Lodico, Spaulding, & Voegtle, 2010). Although it may sound complicated, inter-rater reliability is simply trying to establish agreement between two observers.

In this case, inter-rater reliability would need to be established both in the beginning of the action research studies (baseline) and again in outcome data to determine the effectiveness of the techniques in reducing classroom disturbances. Seeing this as an opportunity to get into the classrooms, the IC should discuss the importance of needing to establish inter-rater reliability. The teacher can serve as one rater and the instructional coach can serve as the other. And voila! The instructional coach is in the classrooms, observing the teachers and the classroom disturbances firsthand. Most important, the instructional coach has established a collaborative environment in which teachers can share, learn from one another, and—most important—test in their classrooms for themselves whether the technique under study is effective or not.

You can see in this example, which uses the classroom field-testing approach, that the instructional coach is truly a facilitator, a "guide on the side" as they often say, and not the dispenser of knowledge. The instructional coach is not coming in, as in the first example, with advice to fix the broken teacher who can't manage his or her classroom and has to send students to the office on a regular basis. This joint partnership is everything that one wants in a learning community. Once inside the resistant teacher's classroom, the instructional coach can directly observe and assess the situation for him- or herself.

Another beneficial component of this model is that it allows the individual teacher, the one who essentially needs to modify his or her teaching practice, the opportunity to see for him- or herself the change that occurs and thus begin to see the connection between implementing the technique and changing his or her practices to include this technique on a daily basis. Experts in the field of professional development and teacher change emphasize the importance of these two components.

It is important to keep in mind that even with establishing inter-rater reliability in the study, an action research study like the one described in Figure 7.1 may not be as rigorous as a behavioral study found in a peer-reviewed research journal. For example, someone with a critical eye might say that the action research study lacks a comparison group, meaning that there is no group of students who were targeted but did not receive the techniques—all the teachers in the group learned about the techniques and implemented them into their classrooms. This is true; however, many times it is not possible in an applied setting such as this to have a comparison group. In some cases, teachers who go to the initial meeting do not follow through with their action research project and do not implement the initiative that is being investigated. In some cases, these teachers' classrooms could be used as a comparison group—those targeted but who did not receive any type of treatment.

Inevitably, it will be important to recognize that classroom field-testing projects conducted by your teaching staff will not have the rigor of research studies that have been done by professional researchers. However, as noted before, that is acceptable, since one of the main goals of doing action research is to give the instructional coaches the opportunity to enter closed-door classrooms and work in assisting teachers to improve their practice.

HOW THE INSTRUCTIONAL LEADERSHIP TEAM CAN SUPPORT ACTION RESEARCH

While it may appear that the IC plays the main role in working with teachers on classroom field-testing projects, it is important that all members of the instructional leadership team (ILT) play their role as well. Presented below are some ways the ILT can support classroom field-testing in their school.

1. *Provide supporting materials.* With the rise in popularity of action research, there is no loss of books, videos, and other information available on action research. School leaders can easily support their staff in this effort by purchasing such materials. Start an action research library where these materials can be housed and easily checked out by interested staff.

2. *Highlight classroom field-testing projects.* It is also easy to support action research projects with your staff by highlighting a research project that you come across and think your staff would be interested in. Perhaps you have had discussions with staff about integrating portfolios in an English Language Arts class or in mathematics. Find an action research study that supports this effort, share it with staff, and have an in-depth discussion about it.

3. *A picture is worth a thousand words.* This old saying is definitely true when it comes to educating your staff on action research. The Internet can be a powerful tool for busy administrators. With a few clicks of your keyboard, you can easily search the Internet for examples, both in text and video. These can serve as excellent examples of action research for

your staff. Sometimes just seeing an action research project from start to finish can be inspiring and can certainly serve as an example to launch an in-depth discussion about instruction and assessment.

4. *Educate yourself on action research.* There is probably no better way to lead than by example. Action research is contagious. If you are interested and excited about action research, your staff is going to become interested in action research as well. In addition, they look to you for guidance and knowledge. Therefore, it is important for you to gain as much knowledge about action research as you can in order to support your staff when they become involved in their projects and need assistance. The strategies and knowledge you gain from this book will serve you well in providing your staff with technical assistance and support so they can carry out their own projects. But don't stop there. Read as much as you can on action research. Attend workshops and conferences on action research. You will learn a tremendous amount and be able to bring home some great examples to share with your staff.

5. *Bring in outside experts.* Sometimes it is important to recognize when the technical assistance that you can provide your staff about action research has reached its limit. In doing so, it might be necessary to bring in an outside consultant to work with your staff. When hiring a consultant, it is important to make sure that you have hired the right person. This is particularly true for action research. Make sure that the person has a background specifically in action research. A consultant who teaches research methods in higher education may have little experience in action research and may bring in an extensive amount of knowledge about applied research methods; however, this may have little application to what you and your staff are interested in studying within a classroom.

6. *Highlight from within.* You might not have to look any further than within your existing staff to identify someone who is engaged in conducting action research. For example, if you observed a teacher who has conducted a similar field-testing project, you might want to have that person share their findings at your next staff meeting. There is no one better to explain to teachers how to go about conducting action research than a colleague who has already experienced it firsthand.

7. *Generate interesting research questions.* In addition to the above, you can also continue to support your staff in this endeavor by continually thinking of new classroom field-testing projects for your teachers to work on. Designate a small notebook specifically for field-testing and keep it on your desk. Then, whenever an interesting research topic comes to mind, all you have to do is jot it down and share it with your staff at your regular meetings.

PRESENTING CLASSROOM FIELD-TESTING PROJECTS

Sharing classroom field-testing projects is critical to their overall success. Whether your staff shares their projects informally or formally, establishing an agreed-upon framework to present them is important and should be done early on in the process.

Professional researchers writing for journals follow a standard template established by the American Psychological Association (APA). Presented below is an outline of this framework for most studies. Because of the large volume of studies being edited and published each year, such a standardized framework is necessary for quality control. Whether you and your staff decide to use a more traditional framework like the one presented below or one that is specifically tailored to your needs, the important thing is to involve your staff as part of the shared decision-making process. A tremendous amount of staff buy-in can be generated just from the act of discussing as a group the different aspects of the framework and deciding on those components that have personal meaning and connection to your school.

Framework Classroom Field Testing Projects

Strategy or Intervention Being Tested

- Be sure that teachers clearly describe the strategy, intervention, or technique that they are testing in their classrooms.

- Have the teachers write a sentence or two about the strategy, intervention, or technique in order to adequately describe it.

- Be sure to also describe the context in which the field-testing is taking place. For example, what topic or area has the class been working on recently? What topic will the strategy, intervention, or technique be integrated into? What does the strategy, intervention, or technique need in order to be used?

Participants and Classroom Context

- Describe the key demographic data for the students in the classroom and the types of students the strategy or intervention is being field-tested with (e.g., total number of students in the class, gender, general vs. special education).

Procedure

- Describe any baseline data that was collected prior to introducing the strategy or intervention into the class or group of students.

- Describe how the strategy or intervention was delivered.

Assessment Tools

- Describe the types of assessments you used to collect data on your students:
  - Informal assessments
  - Formal assessments
  - Video or observations
  - Interviews

Results

- How did you analyze the data?

- What do the analyses of all the types of data tell you?

- Did the technique or strategy make the desired impact on your students' learning?

Reflection

- What did you learn from this experience . . .
  - about the classroom setting?
  - about your students?
  - about yourself as a teacher?
  - about your instruction?

- How will you use what you have learned to improve upon your future effectiveness as a teacher?

Recommendation for Expanding to Other Classrooms

- Would you recommend this technique or strategy to colleagues?

- What needs to occur to expand this into other classrooms and train other teachers about this strategy?
  - Does it require additional training or professional development?
  - Are additional supplies, materials, or equipment needed?

SUMMARY

Traditionally, action research has been used to help teachers isolate strategies and variables that are effective in the classroom and to provide them a framework for integrating these effective practices into their pedagogy. In this chapter, action research takes on a new role as a tool for instructional coaches to use in working with resistant teachers. By establishing a collaborative group, instructional coaches are able to work with teachers within the action research framework as a technical assistant, providing information and content knowledge about action research and various research designs, as well as a second pair of eyes, helping teachers gather more reliable and valid data for their action research projects. This action research technique is very different from just delivering classroom instruction in that the instructional coach is working collaboratively with teachers and the focus of the effort is not on fixing something that is broken in a particular teacher but on studying together the effectiveness of different instructional strategies and techniques that align themselves with creating effective learning environments.

Action research not only helps instructional coaches work with resistant teachers, action research also needs to be supported by the school's administrator. Dedicated time needs to be available for teachers to meet in action research groups with instructional coaches to plan research and analyze their results afterward. When more expertise is necessary to address some of the issues unearthed by the action research, professional development and maybe even some outside technical assistance may be warranted to successfully address the issue. Overall, however, action research can be valuable in bringing individuals together who typically do not work together.

Self-Study Activity #7

Action Research Survey

Name: _____

Date: _____

Subject: _____

Grade level: _____

1. What is a problem or issue related to classroom instruction and student learning/achievement that you would like to address and study?

_____

_____

_____

_____

2. What new practice or intervention do you want to implement into your classroom to address this issue or challenge?

_____

_____

_____

_____

3. What does current research on this new practice or intervention suggest?

_____

_____

_____

_____

_____

4. How will you measure and determine the effectiveness of introducing this new practice or strategy into your classroom?

_____

_____

_____

_____

_____

The ILT's Role in Changing Teacher Practices Buildingwide

8

The ILT's Role in Changing Teacher Practices Buildingwide

8

> **Mrs. Skyler Sanders, School Principal**
> **Journal Entry: January 14**

It took us awhile, but now everything is going well. Our IC has managed to work wonders in the building and has served as an extension of the ILT to fulfill our mission and vision. As the instructional leader of the building, I still believe that the best way to improve student achievement is by providing students with the highest quality of instruction possible, so it troubled me that I wasn't able to provide that level of support to my teachers by getting in and observing classrooms regularly. There was just too much to do. But having an IC changed all of that, and while it took us some time to figure out the most effective way to use her talents, in the end, the ILT and the IC made a perfect and highly effective team.

In past years, when I couldn't get in and observe classrooms every day, I found myself trying to change my teachers' instructional practices in other ways. One method I used was to find research studies in journals and on the Internet. These educational journals provided research support for various instructional strategies and practices that teachers could integrate into their classrooms. At meetings, I would pass out research articles and ask my staff to read them. Occasionally, we would even have a discussion about the study and the results. I thought that providing my staff with proof that these practices worked was enough to get them to change their practices and integrate these strategies; however, in the end, I found this was not the case. Few people actually read the articles, and no one ever tried any of the strategies.

Another method that I have used to try and change teacher practices is to provide teachers and staff with ongoing professional development. I brought in experts from all over the country to present teachers with information on a wide variety of topics. Everyone left the professional development meeting excited and talking about it. I thought that excitement and newfound enthusiasm would spill over into the classroom. But again, this did little to change teacher practices, and while it was expensive, it was not terribly successful.

Mrs. Wright, on the other hand, has had great success working with teachers to improve classroom instruction. This has taken a great deal of careful planning by the ILT and hours and hours of work on Mrs. Wright's behalf. Currently, Mrs. Wright has been working with small, grade-level groups of teachers as well as providing one-to-one classroom sessions. This has been great, but I have been feeling the need now to take it to the next level and try to put something in place that would expand our efforts to something that would be buildingwide.

I brought this idea up at our last ILT meeting and asked Mrs. Wright to begin researching the literature on effective ways to engage teachers in professional development and change their instructional practices. We spend way too much time and money each year on professional development that makes little impact in the classroom. I am excited to see what Mrs. Wright comes up with and how the IC will work with the ILT to build a cohesive learning community within our building.

Mrs. Janice Wright, Instructional Coach
Journal Entry: January 14

I love how my position has really developed here in the building and how all teachers and staff (and the school principal) know my role as the IC. Working with the teachers has been great! I have weekly grade-level meetings with teachers, and I am regularly working with others by pushing into their rooms to observe, model best practices, and provide formative feedback.

Now that we have that under my belt, the ILT and I have started discussing what we can do next to take everything that we have done here a step further. After a nice discussion, we have come to the conclusion that we want to develop some type of model or process to get the professional development that we provide teachers into their classrooms. The ILT asked me to begin the leg work to collect articles and research in this area, and I was happy to do it. I have come across some interesting research and discussion about getting teachers to change their practices and why it is so difficult for many teachers (and other professionals) to adopt and adapt new practices into their professional repertoire. From what I have read, one of the reasons why this has been such a challenge is that professional development often focuses on trying to change teachers' attitudes about the instructional practice first. This is so true! I can't remember all the trainings I sat through in my career where the trainer (usually someone outside the district) came to the school and made a presentation about the intervention or program, and most of the time was spent trying to show us stuff that would convince us of how great it was and how we should use it. There is rarely even an opportunity for teachers to experiment and field-test what they have just learned, nor is there opportunity for teachers to determine or judge whether the new thing is effective and whether or not they want to use it based on field-testing it in their classrooms.

So this is where I think I want to go with this: I think we should implement a professional development model where the ILT selects a series of evidence-based instructional strategies that have solid, rigorous research supporting their use. Next, the ILT supports quality professional development for teachers to learn how to go about using and implementing this new strategy or intervention into their classrooms. The training is then followed up by teachers field-testing these strategies in their classrooms and collecting data to determine if these strategies are indeed effective with their students. In the final step, teachers would later reconvene to present, share, and discuss their field-testing results as well as the future of these evidence-based strategies for their building.

I have been able to find many articles and research on changing teachers' practices. I also found some examples of professional development models that we can use as a foundation for the model we want to create for our building. I have selected the best articles to share directly with members from the ILT and have also put together a short PowerPoint presentation overview of my idea. I really think that we are ready for this now! Maybe we can connect with the local university and make this a joint effort eventually. I'll present this idea to the ILT at our next meeting.

Mr. Colten Stevens, Teacher and ILT
Journal Entry: January 15

At a recent meeting of the ILT, we talked about trying to expand the impact of professional development in the building. Mrs. Wright, our IC, was very helpful in going out and doing the initial leg work for us. She gathered multiple articles on PD and changing teacher practices and presented some ideas for a possible model. I found the model that Mrs. Wright has suggested to be very interesting. First of all, I like the idea that as a building, we are customizing a model to fit our needs. Too many times, we are too quick to take on some other program or idea that worked great someplace else but might not work for us. (In my opinion, that has always been one of the main problems when our school has tried to do anything new to make improvements.) The model that we developed (and will pilot) will allow the teachers at every grade level to test for themselves the various strategies, materials, and resources that we would like them to integrate into their classrooms on a day-to-day basis to improve classroom instruction. These strategies would also be research-based, but in a way, we would be doing our own independent research to see if these strategies work for our teachers and for our students. Then, as a community, we will decide through classroom field-testing whether these strategies work, how they work, and if we want to add them to our list of tested strategies that have been shown to be effective in our building. Later, we hope that teachers will build upon the momentum of this and begin to field-test some additional strategies that they believe work and that we can again field-test within our own learning community. It sounds like a great initiative and one that I really think will breathe some life and excitement back into the many fine teachers we have in the building who, over the years, have felt their talents stifled.

PROFESSIONAL DEVELOPMENT AND CHANGING TEACHER PRACTICES

Professional development (PD) training has been the traditional cornerstone for improving teacher effectiveness and impacting student performance. As shown in Figure 8.1, an underlying premise exists with the use of this model. While it appears almost simplistic in nature, the assumption is that training staff about a particular technique or skill will result in changing their attitudes about the topic. This change in attitude will then result in a change in classroom practice. Finally, this change

Figure 8.1   Traditional Role of Professional Development

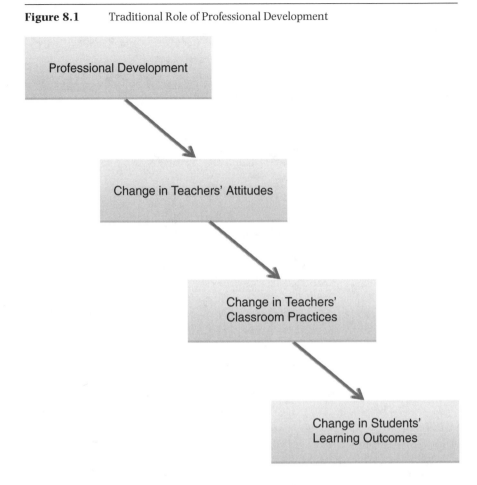

in classroom practice will result in a change in student performance that results in improved student achievement. If this is the case, then why was the professional development provided by the principal in the journal entry above not effective?

As noted by Guskey (2002), the logic behind the professional development model shown in Figure 8.1 is the most popular model used in education today. With origins dating back to a behavioral model from the early 1930s, this model focuses its efforts in trying to first change people's attitudes, believing that an attitudinal shift will eventually evoke a change in teachers' classroom practices, with student outcomes to follow; however, work by Guskey (2002) and other prominent experts in the field suggest something quite different. They have found this model to be ineffective in trying to make real change in teacher practices. Instead, their work suggests that professional development trainers who focus solely on trying to change teacher attitudes first will have (and will continue to have) little impact on making real change in teacher practices.

In his model Guskey (2002) suggests that those planning on implementing professional development not focus on changing attitudes of teachers but instead work on *showing* teachers the benefits to their students when the activity that they learned in professional development is implemented into the classroom. Research on changing teacher practices has also shown that training, articles, and research about the effectiveness of a teaching strategy are not enough to convince teachers to alter their instruction. Teachers care about their students, and their students doing well is a direct reflection of themselves as a teacher (Guskey, 2002). Teachers are not willing to risk changing the strategy they currently use (even though it is ineffective) for a new strategy that they just learned about in a workshop because it might give them even poorer results in their students' performance. In other words, teachers are not willing to risk it all for something that they themselves have no firsthand proof of, even if there is a stack of research articles documenting the effectiveness of the strategy. Therefore, the key to changing teacher practices is to create as close a connection as possible between what was learned in professional development and the immediate gains students make when the new practice is implemented into the classroom. According to Guskey (2002) and others, when teachers see students responding (e.g. learning, getting excited, etc.) to a new teaching strategy that they themselves just learned about in a workshop, the chances of teachers valuing this strategy and increasing the future use of this strategy increase exponentially.

Today, many professional development sessions provide teachers with evidence-based instructional strategies. These strategies have research supporting their use and ability to produce desired results or outcomes with students. However, merely hearing about research and evidence-based strategies is not enough to convince teachers of their value and purpose or to get them to change their current classroom practices. The model that we are proposing incorporates an additional component to a professional development model that allows teachers and staff the opportunity to field-test these evidence-based strategies in their own classrooms to determine for themselves if they are effective and truly work. Then the teachers get back together and share the results or findings from their studies. As a school community, they decide (based on the evidence from their classroom studies) whether or not the instructional strategy or technique under investigation warrants being added to the school's list of evidence-based practices. The catalyst to changing teacher practices with this approach is that the community (i.e., the teachers) gets to test out and decide for itself if these strategies work. However, in participating in the series of classroom studies, these teachers see for themselves the results in the students' learning. And when they see their students learning from these new strategies, they have little reluctance in incorporating these strategies into their daily instructional use.

Training also needs to be very specific and focused. Teachers find professional development training to be of little or no value because the training sessions themselves are too long and too broad. Therefore, it is critical to focus on a specific skill or instructional strategy that you and your staff feel needs to be improved across multiple classrooms. Whether you decide as a team to have in-house staff development (with a teacher training other staff members on the strategy that he or she uses and finds successful in class) or hire an external consultant, the most important part of this component is that it is a shared collaborative decision.

Also, make sure to keep the trainings short. If you are focusing on one strategy or one skill, there is no need to dedicate a full day to it when a half-day or couple of hours would certainly suffice. A series of short, focused trainings is often more effective than one or two full-day sessions. Keeping trainings short and focused also sends a message to your staff that their time is important and that you are acknowledging that fact.

THE ROLE OF THE IC IN CHANGING TEACHER PRACTICES: A BUILDINGWIDE EFFORT

The instructional coach (IC) will play a pivotal role in working to change teacher practices in a large-scale effort. In this process, the IC will once again serve as an extension of the instructional leadership team (ILT) by first working with members of the ILT to develop the framework for the professional development, providing the PD, and working with teachers in their classroom to field-test what they have learned.

STEPS IN ESTABLISHING A LARGE-SCALE EVIDENCE-BASED FRAMEWORK

While the needs for each building are unique, there are some basic steps involved in developing the appropriate framework for the model developed for Mrs. Wright's building. Since the initial success of framework falls heavily upon the shoulders of the ILT and the IC, it is important that members of the ILT are familiar with key steps that should be followed to complete this process. Presented below are these key steps:

Step 1: ILT Needs to Identify What Needs to Be Improved

In this first step, we recommend that the ILT establish a list of evidence-based instructional strategies that they would like teachers

Figure 8.2   Evidence-Based Framework

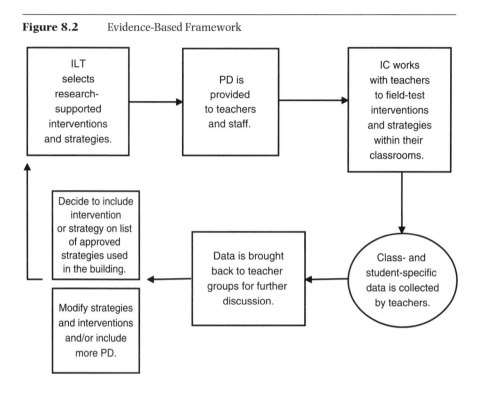

buildingwide to implement more on a daily basis. As shown in Figure 8.2, the IC can assist members of the ILT by helping to gather, review, and consolidate research and information on effective instructional strategies. Initially, these instructional strategies might be more universal in nature and applicable to all teachers. The ILT should use data to determine what strategies need to be more present in the classrooms. Observations of classrooms for a period of time and/or a survey of teachers about the strategies they are currently using as well as those they would like to include or want more information about could also be done. The important part is that there is a basis for the strategies being focused on through the professional development.

Step 2: Determine Type of Training and Who Will Deliver Training

Once the ILT has selected the list of evidence-based strategies or interventions that they want to focus on, the next step is to determine *who* will provide the professional development and *how* will it be provided. In most cases, it is natural to have the IC deliver the training. Depending on the strategies, the IC may also have to receive some training and/or do some research and practice prior to training the teachers and related staff on the evidence-based strategies. In other cases, an outside trainer may have to be hired. In this situation, it is important that the IC learn from the outside trainer so that the IC can replicate the practices afterward when working with the teachers.

Step 3: Implement Professional Development

As noted above, the professional development training also needs to be very specific and focused. Teachers often find professional development training to be of little or no value because the training sessions themselves are too long and too broad. Therefore, it is critical to focus on a specific skill or instructional strategy that you and your staff feel needs to be improved across multiple classrooms. Instead of trying to cover all the strategies or interventions in one PD session, break them across multiple sessions and provide teachers with a schedule of when these sessions will take place.

Last, the principal should also attend training sessions for two reasons: one, to again show support to staff and send the message, "This is important. . . . You are taking time out of your busy day, and I am taking time out of mine," and two, as the principal, you are doing a study to determine the effectiveness of the instructional strategy and therefore need to observe the session to collect quantitative and qualitative data. It is important to collect observational data to insure that the session or training is being delivered correctly, that staff are engaged and learning about the strategy, and that staff are confident that they can go back to their classrooms and implement that strategy.

Step 4: Establish Method of Field-Testing Evidence-Based Practices in the Classroom

As part of the collaborative process, the IC and members of the ILT will also want to develop a process for teachers to field-test the evidence-based practices in their classrooms. In doing so, the teachers and staff will be less likely to feel that things are being imposed on them and more likely to feel that they have more of a role in the process. Have teachers set up a field test that measures how the evidence-based practices work in their classrooms and if they are effective for improving student learning.

Keep Timeline for Field-Testing Short

We have worked with ICs and teachers and have found that the most common mistake both parties make is in selecting a timeline for the field tests that is too long in nature. For example, let's say that a teacher decides to field-test a certain instructional strategy in her classroom. As part of her field test, she decides to examine student achievement on the annual state assessment at the end of the year in order to determine whether the strategy was indeed effective. While this is certainly an interesting idea and one that is commendable, selecting an outcome such as student achievement on a standardized assessment given at the end of the school year is much too far off of a goal for the process to be successful. To make this process effective and truly work to change teacher practices, teachers have to be able to see the connection between the practice that is being field-tested and the outcome—an observable and notable change in their students. The teacher has to be able to make the connection between the two and see it quite clearly before he or she is able and willing to surrender or modify their current instruction.

Unfortunately, a teacher is not going to be able to see such a connection as easily when using a summative measure at the end of the school year. We have found the process to be much more effective in changing teacher practice when the teacher uses a classroom-based assessment—something that teacher commonly uses to assess students' knowledge or ability when teaching that particular topic. For this type of process, it is again important that you and your staff are focused on a specific aspect of instruction and a measurement that provides immediate feedback.

Step 5: Classroom Implementation

Not only is it important for the teacher to select a classroom-based measure, but it is also important that the evidence-based strategy under examination be implemented correctly. Conveying this idea to teachers will allow the IC an opportunity to enter the classroom, observe to see if teachers are implementing the new strategy correctly, and provide just-in-time feedback (and perhaps a little modeling) to the teachers who are field-testing the strategy under investigation.

Including the Resistant Teacher

The field-testing component can be used by the effective IC in order to continue his or her work in caring about, sharing, and supporting promising practices in the classroom. The field-testing of these strategies and interventions by teachers will no doubt provide ICs with more of an opportunity to get into a classroom that they otherwise might not be so welcomed in. Earlier in this book, we discussed some of the challenges faced by ICs when working with the resistant teacher; however, the IC should capitalize on the field-testing to recruit the highly resistant teacher into the process.

If you have a teacher that is resistant, deflect this resistance by not going into his or her classroom to conduct observations for field-testing. This is likely to only create more resistance. Instead, the IC should have a conversation with the resistant teacher. Be sure to note during the conversation the knowledge and expertise this individual has in the classroom. Approach the resistant teacher as a valuable resource for the building and for other teachers. Try to convince the resistant teacher to help you go around and observe other teachers' classrooms as part of the field-testing component. There are lots of benefits to doing this. If the resistant teacher agrees, make sure that you (as the IC) send him or her to observe rooms where the instructional strategy being field-tested could use a little assistance. But also send the teacher to observe classrooms where you know the strategy is being delivered with fidelity. This will allow the teacher to see for him- or herself how the strategy looks when it is delivered correctly and, most important, will allow the teacher the opportunity to see the students excited and motivated when the strategy begins to work for them. Ideally, the IC would want to set up environments where teachers are seeing their own students excited and learning, but in a pinch, a teacher such as this seeing it vicariously in another teacher's classroom is the next best thing for that teacher, who then might take one step closer to changing his or her practices.

As the IC, make sure that you take advantage of debriefing the resistant teacher after he or she has conducted a number of observations. It will start a conversation and help to build trust between the IC and the resistant teacher.

Step 6: Reconvene and Share Data/Results

It is also important that each teacher shares with other teachers his or her own data from students following delivery of the strategy. The ILT needs to support this type of sharing, collaboration, and rich, in-depth discussion by adjusting teachers' schedules so these meetings can be conducted.

Step 7: Determine Whether More Training Needs to Occur and Determine Effectiveness of the Strategy

When the teachers reconvene to discuss their results and data from their classroom field tests, it is important for the IC to determine whether or not additional training needs to occur in order to enhance the fidelity of the strategies or interventions. If this is the case and more training needs to occur, the IC should work with the entire ILT to again plan the additional training and to ensure that it is supported appropriately.

Remember that as a group, you now have data from each of the classrooms where the strategy was implemented to determine whether the strategy was effective. You will want to examine the data from the different classrooms in different ways. Here are some questions to think about when beginning to peruse through your data:

- Was the strategy effective for every student in the classroom?
- Were there students who still had difficulty grasping the concept, even after the new strategy was in place?

- If so, were there any commonalities in these students?
- Did teachers have to make further modifications to the strategy to meet all the students' needs?

THE POWER OF EVIDENCE-BASED CLASSROOM STUDIES

By examining Figure 8.3, you can see that one of the most powerful aspects of this model of professional development is the tremendous amount of data that you receive from it. Where else have you had this much feedback from professional development? If done correctly, this model allows you and your staff to research or test different instructional strategies that you have learned during professional development. More important, the data that are gathered are germane to your students and your school building and culture. Testing the strategy out in different classrooms using an action research design is known in the research world as *replication.* Replication essentially means to recreate a study that has already been conducted to see if the same results can be achieved again. In this situation, the replication is not occurring in the same site over time, but in similar sites (e.g., classrooms in your building) all at the same time, testing the same instructional strategy.

With this particular approach, you and your staff will be able to tell quite easily whether or not a strategy is effective in your setting, with the diverse groups that your teachers have to address. Over time, you and your staff will assemble a large amount of data on the various strategies and on how students react and learn when teachers use them. You may find from your action research that while applied research supports the use of certain instructional strategies, these strategies may be somewhat ineffective for the body of students you are serving in your building.

Figure 8.3 Combining Professional Development and Classroom Field-Testing

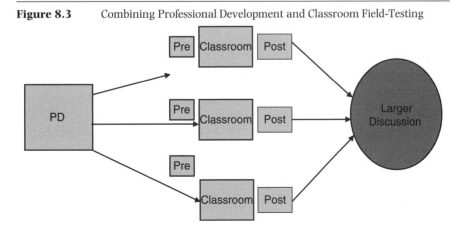

In addition, you may find that in order for these strategies to be effective, certain alterations have to be made as you are working with them. This process helps to inform and offer programmatic refinement for the professional development as well.

SUMMARY

Professional development has been the cornerstone for trying to improve teacher practices in the classroom. However, research on professional development has shown that the majority of professional development training that occurs in schools is ineffective for making any real changes to instruction. Research and studies in this area suggest that professional development should not focus on trying to change teachers' attitudes but should try to show teachers the changes in their students when these practices are implemented in the classroom. Having teachers field-test the instructional practices and interventions they learn about in PD is one method that allows teachers to see for themselves the benefit of using their new knowledge and practices on their students' learning and achievement. If done correctly, teachers will judge for themselves (based on the data they collect in their classrooms) whether or not the evidence-based practice is indeed effective. If it is, they will discuss with others the possibility of adding it to the list of practices supported by the school community. If not, they will have discussions about why this was so and ways that the practice might be modified in order to bring about the desired results. Together, as a community, the teachers and staff will continue to investigate those practices that work in their classrooms with their students to achieve the results that they desire.

A New Coach in Town!

9

The ILT's Role in Training New Instructional Coaches

Mrs. Nancy Johnston, New Instructional Coach
Journal Entry: April 14

What have I done? I cannot quite believe I agreed to this, but I did, and now I am completely in over my head. Our instructional coach took a leave of absence—a last-minute thing because of a family emergency. I've been working with the instructional coach on our school's reading program project, and she and I were just at the beginning stages of a planned action research project related to our science curriculum. I've talked with her a few times about the IC position, and from what I saw, I have to admit that I was starting to consider it as a way for me to change what I've been doing for my entire career without leaving the teaching ranks. I've never wanted to be an administrator, and up to now, I never saw any other way of growing professionally. I'll admit I was starting to consider it, but . . . I was only just beginning to find out about this IC project and position. I never expected to take it on so quickly, if at all.

I'm flattered to have been considered and asked to fill in for this last-minute vacancy. I think I am pleased and excited to have this change in my professional life, but I surely don't feel ready or prepared in any way! All the other ICs had lots of training before this project started. They also went to a series of seminars on instructional leadership at our local college's department of education. I know they have read some books on coaching, too. They get to meet once a month, and it is clear they are supportive of each other. All that is great but . . . I feel like an outsider. I haven't had any training. Ms. Sanders, our principal, gave me the books on coaching, but I haven't had a moment to even skim through them. I don't know most of the other coaches. I went to their last meeting, but I didn't feel like I was up to speed on anything under discussion. At this point, I only know what our IC did here when she worked with me and the other Grade 4 teachers. I have her planning book and I've begun to talk with some of the other teachers here about what they were doing together, but most of them don't know me nearly well enough yet to consider me their coach. I don't know most of them well enough yet to know how to even begin to build the relationships needed in order to keep this collaboration going.

I've meet with the principal twice. She shared a lot about how the instructional leadership team worked. She also told me a bit about what they had learned from this project so far. I know her pretty well, but this is a new professional relationship and I have to work carefully to build it right. She and our former IC seemed to make a great team, and I am worried about being able to fit in as her new ILT partner.

I don't know who to call or where to turn beyond our school. I guess I'll just have to trust my instincts, read Mrs. Wright's notes carefully, and start building my own bridges with the principal and the faculty. I can do that. I'll have to do that. I just wish I had a mentor or at least some time to study and to plan. Right now, my goals are to survive until June, do the best I can to keep this going, and figure out whether or not this is something for me to pursue for the future. I've decided to start by addressing those areas where I feel I have some level of expertise and work from there. I am going to focus on reading and on classroom management for now and see where it all goes from here.

I am also going to stop asking myself what was I thinking? *and start asking* what should I be doing? *Hopefully the answers to both will come soon.*

WHAT HAS HAPPENED HERE?

As the instructional leadership team (ILT) continues and moves forward, it would be great to keep the same crew together throughout its entirety. The group that went through all the training and planning and first mistakes and course corrections together is the best group to continue on, building on success and learning from missteps and from evidence gathered. However, that only happens in a perfect world. Despite the best intentions and planning of all involved, selecting coaches who are committed to the program, and finding leaders who plan to stay put for a while as the team develops, life often intervenes. In this case, the instructional coach (IC) had every intention of staying with this program, but it was not to be. With little notice and less preparation, a new coach has come on board: someone who hasn't had the benefit of the training and planning; who hasn't yet built relationships with faculty, with fellow coaches, and with the principal; who hasn't had time to readjust her role within her school community; and who has to pick up the story while it is already in progress.

This new coach is battling many mixed emotions. She is aware of her lack of preparation for this role. At times, she feels isolated from her fellow coaches and at a loss as to what to do next in order to keep the project moving forward. She does know that she has her limitations, but she is willing to find out more and to resist the urge to head for the hills. This is a moment where everyone—the ILT and all the other ICs in the district—has to take on yet another new role: coach for the coach!

WHAT SHOULD EVERYONE DO?

First, *stay calm* and try to focus on the first and most essential needs of the coach, the ILT, and the school. The building principal needs to take the lead and find some time for this new IC to meet with her, the faculty, and her fellow coaches. A short-term plan should be first on the agenda. Once the new IC is feeling a bit more confident, a modified training program can continue without a major time commitment from anyone involved. This is going to be a learn-as-you-go practicum on coaching, and everyone will have to be prepared for some role expansion, adjustment, and redefinition.

Everyone needs to keep their sense of humor and stay focused on the goals of the project. Everyone involved needs to act based on past practice and new information and not on assumption. Easy? No! Possible? Absolutely! Necessary? Yes, indeed!

THE GAME PLAN: GET STARTED RIGHT AWAY!

These are some first-step suggestions to be taken in training a new coach:

• *Sit down and talk.* The principal and the new IC need to do a brief review of what has happened and what is planned. The new IC in our example is already part of the ILT, so a goal review shouldn't be new for her. The principal can talk in general terms about how this team worked with the former IC but should leave the door open to new ideas and perceptions from this new IC. This is also a great chance to begin a new conversation about the whole ILT project, as the principal now has an IC who can bring the perspective of the faculty to the discussion. It is important at this initial meeting to open up many avenues for communication (e-mail, phone calls, notes, etc.) and to encourage as much communication as possible from both team members.

• *Find a player/coach.* Reach out to the other principals and ICs in district and see if there is someone who would be a good and willing candidate to coach the coach, to be a player/coach. Work out a schedule so the new IC can spend several days early on shadowing and meeting with her mentor coach. This will help set the general parameters for the new position without dictating the specifics of the requirements for the school involved. It also helps the new IC make a connection with someone in the IC group so that she doesn't feel like such an outsider at district meetings.

The player/coach and the new IC should set up a regular schedule for e-mail or phone dialogue so that there is a built-in lifeline for getting answers to questions, locating resources, and initial planning assistance.

- *Set up a day where the new IC, along with her mentor coach, can visit district personnel who serve as resources for the building projects.* Meeting with subject area coordinators and pupil personnel staff (PPS; any ancillary staff that may be involved with the student, such as special ed. teachers/paras, speech therapy teachers/paras, guidance counselors, social workers, and anybody else involved in the education of the students) provides an opportunity to update the new IC on projects already in progress, to discuss new developments in these districtwide areas, and to begin the conversation about how the new IC can access these resources.

- *Schedule several planning sessions for the new IC and the school principal.* Set aside time at the next faculty meeting to reintroduce this faculty member in her new role to the rest of the ILT and to begin a new conversation in this reconstituted ILT.

- *Provide the new IC with copies of all research material, books, and data that was earlier shared with all ICs.* Schedule a series of meetings over the first several months to discuss each of these items. This can be done by the building principal, the player/coach, or both, as needed.

- *Plan together to begin the new IC's activities at the school.* Select one or two projects with which the new IC is most familiar, and add on others as progress and time allow until the IC activities at the school are back at full swing and the IC is no longer thought of as the new IC but rather as a full member of the ILT.

These steps, taken as soon as possible, will help the new IC feel more prepared for this new adventure. He or she will soon be up to speed with all the training and planning that has gone before and will, with his or her mentor IC and ILT's help, quickly become part of the district IC family.

PLAYER/COACH: MENTOR COACHING 101

Coaching the coach can be very similar to coaching the teacher, but it can also be very different! In many ways, the theory is exactly the same. Coaching one's peers at every level requires ability to

- assess the level of coaching need and receptivity.
- diagnose without evaluating.
- reinforce best practice.

- encourage data collection and analysis.
- respond to needs in ways that promote growth.
- encourage collaboration.
- facilitate coaching assistance from other sources.
- procure resources.
- keep all ILT members focused on the goals defining academic achievement at the highest level. However, in mentoring new coaches, there are some differences and some additional requirements.

Here are some other items to keep in mind as well:

- New coaches are, by definition, receptive to assistance and advice. If not, then how can they possibly provide the same service for others?
- New coaches will need advice on facing challenges not typical of their previous experiences in the classroom. This is especially challenging without the foundation of training, dialogue, planning, and support experienced by the current cadre of ICs.
- New coaches have a finite amount of time in which to learn an almost infinite amount of information and to acquire the basic skills necessary for success in this new role. Their mentor must compress a lot of information and advice into a short time frame so that the new coach can get started in this new role as soon as possible.
- Much of the mentoring can be accomplished via shadowing, conversation, e-mails, and phone calls. Unlike the role of coaching teachers, this type of mentoring becomes more distant over time as the new IC spends more and more of his or her day and week at his or her own school. After the initial intensive training sessions and shadowing opportunities, much of the remaining mentoring over time becomes a matter of planned and scheduled conversations at greater and greater intervals.
- The new coach doesn't know the team. The player/coach must build the bridge between the new IC and her IC peers. As this bridge is built, the mentor will begin to move from a singular coaching role to part of a collaborative team of mentor coaches.

Becoming a mentor to a new IC is definitely an additional responsibility. It is yet another new trail the team has to blaze together. It isn't easy, but there are benefits that come with this new role that make it worthwhile for everyone involved.

WHAT'S IN IT FOR ME? BENEFITS OF THE NEW MENTOR COACH ROLE

With all the demands on an IC's time, why is it a good idea to agree to mentor a new coach? Aside from the obvious professional commitment that coaches share in helping everyone to achieve success, why is this a good thing to take on? Yes, it is always good to model best practices. Allowing another IC to shadow you while you provide a model for coaching is visible affirmation to your own faculty that you believe in the benefit of collaboration, modeling, and mentoring. Yes, it is true that in a helping profession like ours, helping feels good and it is the right thing to do! Yes, all that is true . . . but beyond that, what is in it for the player/coach?

There are some benefits that might not be intuitively obvious at first glance. No matter whether the mentor is the principal of the building or another IC, there are reasons why serving in this additional role is a benefit rather than just another obligation. Here are just a few:

1. Working with a new IC who has recently served the ILT as a teacher gives new perspectives of the project from the point of view of the practitioner in the classroom. Instructional coaches can certainly take steps to improve their own practice in light of new insights from this particular ILT member who has been on the other end of the teacher/coach equation.

2. As the mentor meets with the new IC to examine past training, research, and information, what has been learned is reviewed and refreshed and renewed in his or her mind. New discussions of past studies allow the mentor to reinforce some ideas and rethink others. At the end of these sessions, the new IC has a better foundation in understanding this new role, and the mentor has a renewed sense of knowing what has been studied in the past.

3. The new IC has fresh ideas, innovative ways of thinking about current practice, a different way of looking at the IC position, and additional understandings about the needs, concerns, and strengths of colleagues. These new insights can help recalibrate and redefine the school's plans for academic success as needed. This new role for a current member of the building ILT could bring with it important advice and counsel at a crucial point in the school year.

4. The new IC could become your most supportive and valuable partner. This could be a collaboration that helps you to hone your skills as an instructional leader and may better equip you to meet the challenges and overcome the obstacles ahead.

ADVICE FROM THE FIELD: TIPS FROM CURRENT INSTRUCTIONAL COACHES

We asked a group of instructional coaches working in the third year of their ILT effort what tips they would offer to a new coach. Here is what they told us:

1. Start with a teacher who you know who will invite you in . . . even if it's just for a visit at first.

2. Leave a thank-you note in the mailbox of each teacher with whom you visit during the first few weeks of your new role. Affirmation is important. Perhaps you might also leave a little treat, such as a piece of chocolate, to brighten your colleague's day.

3. Volunteer to work first with a small group of students to demonstrate a skill or technique that falls within your comfort zone.

4. Be available to listen. Make yourself visible in the hallways and the faculty room.

5. Study the curriculum and assessment materials in use at your building so that you are confident and familiar with them when assisting teachers in their use.

6. Schedule time with teachers to go into classrooms. They are more likely to welcome you when your visit is planned in advance.

7. Send out a form that asks teachers if they need help with anything specific. That will give you an invitation of sorts into many classrooms. Once invited in, you can build on that relationship and really begin your coaching mission.

EVERYONE WINS: COACHING THE COACH SHARPENS EVERYONE'S GAME

We never know where inspiration and collaboration will come from. By extending a hand to help this new IC, instructional leaders could be providing for themselves the coach they will need to make them even more effective and successful. By coaching the coach, leaders have a hand in bringing a new voice to the discussion, a new resource to the effort, and another opportunity for everyone on the ILT to be better! By volunteering to fill in as the new IC, educators can expand their roles and grow professionally without leaving the ranks of teaching. This new development, even if it comes unplanned, could be a great fit to the students in your district and a wonderful way to strengthen the team. If asked to become a coach or to coach a coach, our advice is *go for it!*

Toolbox for the Instructional Coach

10

Examples of Surveys, Protocols, and Tools

Parent Survey

Please take a moment to answer each of these questions. Please use as much detail as possible.

1. Three things I really like about this school are . . .

2. One thing I wish I could change about our school is . . .

3. My greatest hope for my child this year in school is . . .

Teacher Survey

Please take a moment to answer each of these questions. Please use as much detail as possible.

1. Three things I really like about this school are . . .

2. One thing I wish I could change about this school is . . .

3. My greatest hope for my students this year in school is . . .

Workshop Training Teacher Survey

Criteria	SD					SA
Overall, I found the workshops to be beneficial.	1	2	3	4	5	6
I found the materials provided during the workshops to be helpful.	1	2	3	4	5	6
I found the workshop trainers to be knowledgeable about the instructional strategy or issue being presented.	1	2	3	4	5	6
I thought the workshop provided information about the strategy from the perspective of teachers and staff.	1	2	3	4	5	6
Overall, all my questions were answered.	1	2	3	4	5	6
Overall, I felt responsive to the training.	1	2	3	4	5	6
I feel interested and eager to implement what I have learned.	1	2	3	4	5	6
I feel ready to collect and share data on the strategy that I have just learned about.	1	2	3	4	5	6

Note: 1 = Strongly Disagree; 2 = Disagree; 3 = Slightly Disagree; 4 = Slightly Agree; 5 = Agree; 6 = Strongly Agree.

Professional Development Planning Sheet

What in the classroom(s) needs to be improved upon?	What type of training is needed?	Who will present this training?

IC Planning Sheet #1

1. How much of your day is spent in the classroom, observing teaching strategies and student learning?

2. How do you measure success? How *often* do you measure success on specific goals?

3. When you visit a classroom, how can you determine the level of coaching need and the level of coaching receptivity?

4. What constitutes good (effective) communication? How can you promote more effective communication with all faculty members? How can you make sure the communication between the principal, the instructional coach, and the instructional leadership team is effective and consistent?

5. Is your daily presence in all classrooms routine? Expected? Welcomed? If not, what can you do today and in the future to make it so?

6. When you visit a classroom, what three things are you looking for or hoping to accomplish? It is always good to have a plan for the focus of your day.

7. What feedback is provided to teachers from instructional coaching activities?

8. When you visit classrooms, can you tell who is actively involved in the learning process? Can you also tell who is not involved? What can you do to make the answer to the first question "everyone" and to make the second question unnecessary?

IC Planning Sheet #2

In order to check your progress as the instructional coach (IC), it is important for you to reflect on what you and the instructional leadership team (ILT) have accomplished as well as where you still want to go. Take a moment to think about and reflect upon each item below. You may also want to give these questions to members of the ILT (where appropriate).

1. Is *data* a positive or negative word at your school? Why? If it is negative, what can you do to turn that around? That is to say, how can you help teachers to view data as an effective tool to use in informing their instructional decisions on a daily basis?

2. How often in your school day do you ask yourself and others, "How do you know?"? How often are you asked the same question by other members of the ILT?

3. What are five ways to follow up on classroom visits in constructive ways to promote effective instructional decision making and support good practice?

4. Where do the following strategies fit into your instructional leadership/coaching plan?

- suggestions
- feedback
- modeling
- solicitation of opinions
- strategy exploration support
- recruitment of additional resource personnel
- collaboration
- recognition

5. Who is on the ILT in your building? Who is not yet on the team? How can you make sure everyone joins the team? What is the team's purpose and primary goal at your school?

6. How can faculty meetings be organized to support instructional leadership team's efforts?

7. What are three things the ILT can do today to support new initiatives at your school?

8. How do you make sure your faculty and students recognize, acknowledge, and celebrate all the wonderful and positive aspects of your school and your district?

9. What positive message does your instructional leadership role include today?

IC Planning Sheet #3

1. Who is struggling? How can you help turn struggle into success?

2. What data have you collected lately to use while working on short-term goals or to discover the causes of a specific problem or to measure the success of a specific intervention?

3. Does everyone on the faculty get a chance to lead in some way? If not, how can you expand the instructional leadership team (ILT) so that everyone has a chance to lead and a chance to follow?

4. How can you make sure every faculty member takes on a coaching role in some way? How can everyone become more reflective about their own coaching needs?

5. Are your faculty meetings focused primarily on instructional issues or management issues? How can these meetings be used for effective professional development and for action research opportunities?

6. How routine are your communications with faculty, with parents, and with the wider school community? How often are you telling the story of your school's progress?

7. What new piece of data did you find and collect today? How can it be shared and used to make progress toward your school's goals?

8. What is your definition of leadership? Who leads at your school? Who else might be able to lead? How can leadership be shared in ways that are effective for all?

9. Are you more likely to be in your office or out and about in your school every day?

10. Are you leading or managing?

11. How often do *you* reach out for help, support, and advice? What other resources could you invite to help out?

IC Planning Sheet #4

1. Does your school have an active partnership with an area business? Often, opportunities for a great deal of support and for additional resources (both volunteer and financial) are just waiting to be invited to the table by the instructional leadership team (ILT).

2. Where is the instructional leadership role reflected in your Parent-Teacher Organization (PTO) meeting agenda? How might parents be invited to become members of the ILT?

3. What are you going to focus on today and in the future as you visit classrooms? What will your positive message be for today? For the future?

4. How can students become instructional leaders at your school? How can they become action researchers, planning for their own academic progress?

5. What are you planning to do today and in the future to support the literacy programs at your school?

6. What could your school do to focus on test-taking terms across disciplines so that students will have a better understanding of what they are being asked to do on these exams?

7. How can you structure your day around instructional leadership activities and still provide the flexibility required to address the unexpected events that always arise?

8. Have you considered inviting district coordinators to faculty meetings to clarify issues and to learn more about specific curriculum topics?

9. Is there a time at every faculty meeting to hear the concerns of the students? Where is their opportunity to be part of the ILT and to provide input?

10. Where is the next challenge coming from, and how can you be prepared before it arrives?

■ ■ ■

IC Planning Sheet #5

1. What are the top five things that compete for your time each day? What are your top five priorities? How can you make these two lists identical?

2. When is the last time you sent an e-mail to your supervisors detailing some of the most recent accomplishments at your school? It is OK to brag a bit when you have all done wonderful work.

3. How can you help your faculty look at challenges through a different, more positive lens? How can you turn these challenges into opportunities for collaboration, team development, and progress?

4. What success are you celebrating today at your school? What success should your school be celebrating this week? How can you best build on previous success?

5. Who or what dictates your agenda today? Are there things under your control in deciding how your day will be spent that you could take hold of proactively? If not, how can you establish greater control over your daily schedule?

6. What issues has your instructional leadership team identified, researched, addressed, and changed together in the last three months? What issues could you research, act on, and resolve between now and the end of the school year?

7. What have you done today to keep everyone motivated and focused on the mission?

8. Whose voice wasn't heard at your last faculty or grade-level meeting? How can you encourage the reluctant to speak up and get more involved? How can you make the environment safe so that they will take the risk and step into the discussion?

9. Whose accomplishments have you affirmed today? Has everyone had the opportunity for recognition this year?

10. When was the last time you asked for the students' opinions, advice, or suggestions?

11. As the school year ends, what can you and your ILT do to make sure you make the most of the last two or three months in an effort to improve academic instruction? How can you make sure these efforts don't fade?

12. What is happening in every classroom today to further the school's effort to improve students' literacy skills?

13. How can you keep the coaching concept in your school? How can you plan now to continue the forward momentum?

14. When was the last time you stopped to acknowledge your own efforts and successes? Who at your school helps you to affirm the positive each day?

IC Planning Sheet #6

1. How can parents and community leaders coach the faculty and join the instructional leadership team (ILT)?

2. Questions for faculty meetings:

- What works?
- What hasn't worked?
- How can we let go of the things that are not working?
- What is our plan to preserve our progress and keep moving, despite setbacks?
- Who is on our ILT?
- Why isn't everyone on the ILT?
- What issues have been the most divisive for our faculty?
- How can we begin to resolve them so they don't prevent us from moving forward?

3. Questions for the end of the school year: What are three things we learned this year that we did not know before about our school, our faculty, and our students? What are three new things each of us has learned this year about our own instructional leadership style and approach? How can we use all this information to keep our school moving forward academically as the next school year begins?

4. At the end of the day, what is important for our school and our children? How can we make sure we are better today as educators than we were yesterday and that tomorrow we will be even more effective?

Needs Assessment Survey

The following items are designed to gather information from you regarding your current knowledge level about school-related topics. Please read each item carefully and respond using the agreement scale provided below by placing an "X" in the corresponding box.

	Strongly Disagree	Disagree	Slightly Disagree	Slightly Agree	Agree	Strongly Agree
I am knowledgeable about how to handle an emergency/crisis in a school building.						
I am knowledgeable about how a school leader helps develop a school culture and community.						
I am well-versed in how to effectively supervise adults in a school building.						
I am well-versed in how to effectively supervise students in a school building.						
I am knowledgeable about curriculum mapping.						
I am confident that I could use data to guide buildingwide instruction.						
I am confident that I can work directly with teachers using *their* classroom data to help guide *their* classroom instruction.						

I am knowledgeable about using formative assessments to improve instruction and student learning.			
I am knowledgeable about using summative assessments to improve instruction and student learning.			
I am confident that I could develop a professional learning community in a school building.			
I am knowledgeable about professional development and how to lead a professional development series.			
I have effective communication skills for reaching out and working with the community.			
I have effective communication skills for reaching out and working with parents.			
I am knowledgeable about accountability measures.			
I keep up-to-date on current educational news, issues, events, and mandates.			

Promising Practices Building Survey

This survey has been developed to gather information from you regarding your teaching strategies.

Name: _____

Building name: _____

Grade level: _____

What is something related to instruction that you feel you do particularly well?

Would you be willing to serve as a model classroom for other teachers to visit? __ Yes __ No

What is something related to assessments that you feel you do particularly well?

Would you be willing to serve as a model classroom for other teachers to visit? __ Yes __ No

What is a practice that you would like to observe in a model classroom?

References

Green, R. L. (2010). *The four dimensions of principal leadership: A framework for leading 21st century schools.* Boston, MA: Allyn & Bacon.

Guskey, T. (2002). Professional development and teacher change. *Teachers and Teaching: Theory and Practice, 8*(3/4).

Guthrie, J. W., & Schuermann, P. (2010). *Leading schools to success: Constructing and sustaining high-performing learning cultures.* Thousand Oaks, CA: Sage.

Joyce, B., Showers, B., Murphy, C., & Murphy, J. (1989). School renewal as cultural change. *Educational Leadership, 47*(3), 70–77.

Killion, J., & Harrison, C. (2006). *Taking the lead: New roles for teachers and school-based coaches.* Oxford, OH: National Staff Development Council.

Knight, J. (2007). *Instructional coaching: A partnership approach to improving instruction.* Thousand Oaks, CA: Corwin.

Lodico, M. G., Spaulding, D. T., & Voegtle, K. H. (2010). *Methods in educational research: Theory to practice* (2nd ed.). San Francisco, CA: Jossey-Bass.

Makibbin, S. S., & Sprague, M. M. (1993). *The instructional coach: A new role in staff development.* Dallas, TX: National Staff Development Council.

Marzano, R. J., Waters, B., & McNulty, B. A. (2005). *School leadership that works: From research to results.* Denver, CO: Mid-continent Research of Education and Learning (McREL).

Samuels, C. A. (2008). Managers help principals balance time. *Education Week, 27*(23), Retrieved from http://www.edweek.org/ew/articles/2008/02/13/23 sam_ep.h27.html

Saphier, J., & West, L. (2010). How coaches can maximize student learning. *Phi Delta Kappan, 91*(4), 46–50.

Stiggins, R., and Duke, D. (2008). Effective instructional leadership requires assessment leadership. *Phi Delta Kappan, 90*(4), 285–291.

Index

CORWIN
A SAGE Company

The Corwin logo—a raven striding across an open book—represents the union of courage and learning. Corwin is committed to improving education for all learners by publishing books and other professional development resources for those serving the field of PreK–12 education. By providing practical, hands-on materials, Corwin continues to carry out the promise of its motto: **"Helping Educators Do Their Work Better."**

learningforward
Advancing professional learning for student success

Learning Forward (formerly National Staff Development Council) is an international association of learning educators committed to one purpose in K–12 education: Every educator engages in effective professional learning every day so every student achieves.